"Dan Millman captures the essence of the new sports movement and makes it available to a wide popular audience. *Body Mind Mastery* makes it clear that everybody is an athlete and that there is a sport for everybody."

— George Leonard
Author of *The Ultimate Athlete* and *The Life We Are Given*

"Dan Millman has written a superb book . . . more than just another exercise manual. This is a well-organized, clearly written guide for the growing numbers of people who are seeking to achieve optimal levels of health, vitality, and performance in regard to all aspects of life . . . must reading for anyone interested in preventive health, physical fitness, or human potential."

— Ken Dychtwald, Ph.D.
Author of *Bodymind* and *Age Wave*

"Millman's book is a solid, sensible, useful volume for those of us who are unwilling to become professional athletes but who are willing to be healthier and live longer. He understands that the mind is in the body and that the body is in the mind."

— Jim Fadiman, Ph.D.
Psychologist, Lecturer
Stanford University and
California Institute of Transpersonal Psychology

Body
Mind
Mastery

Training for Sport and Life

Body
Mind
Mastery

Training for Sport and Life

Dan Millman

New World Library
Novato, California

New World Library
14 Pamaron Way
Novato, CA 94949

Cover design: Big Fish
Cover illustration: *Proportions of the Human Figure* by Leonardo da Vinci
Text design and layout: Terragraphics, Berkeley, California
Exercise photos of Dan Millman: Tony Iadavaia, Photography Unlimited

Library of Congress Cataloging-in-Publication Data
Body mind mastery : training for sport and life / Dan Millman.
   p.   cm.
Rev. ed. of: The inner athlete. c1994
ISBN 978-1-57731-094-5 (alk. Paper)
      Athletics—Psychological aspects. 2. Physical fitness—Psychological
      aspects. 3. Success. I. Millman, Dan. Inner athlete.
GV706.4.M53 1999   98-53429
796'.01—dc21   CIP

First printing, April 1999
ISBN 978-1-57731-094-5
Printed in Canada on acid-free paper
Distributed to the trade by Publishers Group West

20 19 18

To those who live in the moment of truth,
who confront their fears and never stop dreaming,
who strive for body mind mastery
whether or not they make the varsity team

Contents

Acknowledgments

My deepest appreciation to the following people who contributed, directly or indirectly, to this book: my parents, Herman and Vivian Millman, for their love and support; my past coaches, Xavier Leonard, Ernest Contreras, and Harold Frey, who helped me more than they will ever know; my teammates, for their friendship and support; and the body mind masters East and West who lighted the way and on whose shoulders I stand.

Special thanks to Alfie Kohn, author of *No Contest: The Case Against Competition*, and *Women's Sports and Fitness* magazine for their kind permission to excerpt Dr. Kohn's work; and to John Robbins, author of *Diet for a New America*, whom I've used as a resource.

Deep appreciation to Jason Gardner and the staff at New World Library for their initiative and enthusiasm in creating the finest edition ever of this book.

Finally, every book I write reflects the love, support, and patience of my family.

Body Mind Mastery in the Arena of Daily Life

In each of us are heroes;
speak to them and they will come forth.
— Anonymous

The announcer's voice quivers with excitement as the video begins to play: "Ladies and gentlemen, you are about to see a feat performed for the first time by David Seale — a feat requiring total concentration, daring, and coordination. What you are about to observe did not happen overnight but was the result of months of preparation. Here he goes!"

A figure appears on the screen. David looks relaxed and confident, about to begin a complex series of movements and balances. He stands momentarily poised on the brink; then, with eyes locked straight ahead, his mind focused completely on the task at hand, he begins to move. His body remains relaxed as he engages the first move.

Suddenly, with a tremor, he starts to fall. Quickly, David catches himself, and without wasting a moment on anger or fear stands again and continues toward his goal, his face serene yet concentrated.

As he nears the goal David has another near miss but again regains his balance. He reaches out, his face beaming. After a final moment of suspense, those watching breathe out and applaud with delight as ten-month-old David Seale, master athlete, grasps his mother's outstretched arms. Recorded by his father's camcorder, David has walked his first steps across the living room rug.

You, too, were a body mind master in infancy: your mind focused on the present moment, free of concern or anxiety; your body relaxed, sensitive, elastic, and aligned with gravity; your emotions spontaneous and uninhibited. Even now, you contain the potential for body mind mastery. Within you, a natural athlete is waiting to be born.

We begin life with nearly unlimited potential. But then we lose touch with many of our childhood skills, through limiting beliefs, emotional conflict, and physical tensions. *Body Mind Mastery* provides the means to reclaim your clarity, serenity, and power — creating success not only in the realm of sports but in the larger game of life.

Introduction

The short lives of the laurel wreaths worn by the ancient Olympic champions remind us that victory is fleeting, that moments of glory quickly fade. Even those who shine in their chosen field still confront the challenges of everyday life — relationships, study, and career. What approach to training best prepares us for emotional and psychological challenges in the arena of daily life?

In our tunnel-vision quest for competitive excellence, scores, statistics, and victories too easily become the goal of training. But by focusing too much on striving, we too easily forget *why* we're striving — to experience the satisfaction of stretching ourselves toward our full potential. Our sport or game can become a path to a greater goal or larger contest, a doorway to personal growth, a bridge to our fullest human potential. This book helps us build such a bridge.

I wrote *Body Mind Mastery* to share my insights from decades of world-class training, research, observation, intuition, and teaching — to illuminate the spiritual benefits of any form of skill training, be it sports, dance, music, or martial arts. Whether you are a world-class competitor, weekend athlete, or fitness enthusiast, this book will help you overcome self-created hurdles and reawaken the natural athlete — the body mind master — inside you. *Body Mind Mastery* provides a clear map to a less stressful, more meaningful approach to practicing sport *and* life. It's not about dedicating your life to your training but about dedicating your training to your life.

Athletes — Body and Mind

Webster's Dictionary defines an athlete as "one who engages or competes in exercises or games of physical agility, strength, endurance, etc." The arena of body mind mastery has far broader significance and scope. You can develop mental and emotional qualities that, unlike specialized physical skills, apply to every facet of your life at work and at home.

In *Body Mind Mastery* I use examples from traditional sports such as golf, tennis, running, gymnastics, martial arts, football, and basketball, but these principles apply equally to any form of training.

You don't usually think of musicians or artists as athletes; yet nearly all of them show the same courage, mental focus, and highly coordinated physical skills demonstrated by those who devote the same long hours to sports training. Dancers are among the hardest-working athletes, even though they seldom engage in formal competition.

Aspiring experts in athletics focus on physical development; aspiring *masters* place equal emphasis on developing body, mind, and emotions in order to achieve balance. You may or may not seek competitive glory, but the qualities you develop in your chosen form of training can, if approached correctly, breed success in every facet of daily life.

The first step to body mind mastery is the recognition that your relationships, health, career, family, and finances are all the "events" of daily life — like the 100-meter hurdle or the parallel bars. Success in this larger arena is not measured in scores or win/loss records but in a newfound sense of meaning, purpose, direction, and connection.

Training, Inside Out

You are a dynamic whole greater than the sum of your parts. By integrating your body, mind, and emotions through training, you reshape your life.

Training is a mirror of your life that reflects both your weaknesses and strengths as you hike up the path to your potential. At the highest level, as you enter the *zone* — the moment of truth — training has the power to lift your spirits to a higher plateau so that you experience life in a new way — a way that will become clear as your journey continues.

I use the terms *training* and *practice* interchangeably as the intention and commitment to improve or refine a skill. Body mind mastery, however, transcends skill improvement for its own sake; rather, it can be a path and process to develop a balanced body, mind, and spirit.

The musician practices music, the athlete practices athletics, the body mind master practices *everything*.

You may practice a sport, but do you still practice handwriting, or walking, or breathing? How often do you fully engage yourself in each daily task, whether walking or washing the dishes, in order to fully experience the potential of each moment? This awareness is a reward far richer than any fleeting victory.

My Discoveries About the Larger Arena

As a collegiate gymnast, several key insights shaped my approach to practice and teaching. After winning a world championship and coaching an NCAA Champion and top U.S. Olympian, I decided I was onto something.

In the process of teaching and coaching, I noticed that athletes' problems learning or improving were tied to weak fundamentals. To raise their potential — their *talent quotient* — athletes needed to rebuild their foundations for success: strength, suppleness, stamina, coordination, balance, rhythm, timing, and reflex speed. This understanding led me to great success as a gymnast and coach.

At the same time I observed in my own life that my ability to do handstands and somersaults didn't help much when I went out on a date. Nor were these skills useful when I got married, had children, faced financial issues, or confronted the hundreds of other challenges in everyday life. This realization catalyzed a search for *the fundamentals necessary to create success not just in sport but in daily life.*

For athletes, scores, performance times, or win-loss records often serve as the primary measure of success. Movement skills, themselves, have little application in daily life, but the internal qualities you develop through these activities — mental focus, emotional energy, and the ability to relax the body under stress — can improve the quality of every moment.

Today, some Olympic ski jumpers warm up with T'ai Chi Ch'uan and Aikido masters teach golf clinics. Eastern cultures have always known that mind training is essential for physical success. We are only now coming to realize that each culture, with its rich diversity of language and beliefs, contributes to the well-being of the whole. Our potential will blossom in the sunlight of deeper awareness. The time has come to awaken the body mind master — the peaceful warrior — within each of us.

— *Dan Millman*
San Rafael, California
Spring 1999

Body
Mind
Mastery

Creating Success in Sport and Life

PART ONE

Understanding the Larger Game

Training, the heart of the athletic experience, can be represented by a journey up a mountain path. The peak represents your highest potential. Wherever you stand on your path, it is wise to have a clear map of the terrain ahead — a way of seeing your position in relation to your goals, a view of upcoming hurdles, and an understanding of the effort required to reach the peak.

Realistic vision, a deep awareness of your potential in a given endeavor, enables you to choose the wisest course and to train for it. From a good beginning, all else flows.

CHAPTER ONE

Natural Laws

Nature's way is simple and easy,
but men prefer what is intricate and artificial.
— Lao Tzu

For fifteen years I trained with great energy in the sport of gymnastics. Even though I worked hard, progress often seemed slow or random, so I set out to study the process of learning. Beginning with standard psychological theory, I read studies of motivation, visualization, hypnosis, conditioning, and attitude training. My understanding grew, but only in bits and pieces. Reading Eastern philosophy, including the traditions of Taoist and Zen martial arts, expanded my knowledge, but I still lacked the understanding I sought.

Eventually, I turned to my own intuitive experience for the answers. I understood that infants learn at a remarkable pace compared to adults. I watched my little daughter Holly at play, to see if I could discover what qualities she possessed that most adults lacked.

One Sunday morning as I watched her play with our cat on the kitchen floor, my eyes darted from my daughter to the cat and back again, and vision began to crystallize; an intuitive concept was forming in my mind about the development of talent — not just physical talent but emotional and mental talent as well.

I noticed that my young daughter's approach to play was as relaxed and mindless as the cat's, and I realized that the essence of talent is not so much a presence of certain qualities but rather an *absence* of the mental, physical, and emotional obstructions most adults experience.

After that discovery I found myself taking long walks alone, observing the forces of wind and water, trees and animals — their relationship to the earth. At first, I noticed only the obvious — that plants tend to grow toward the sun, that objects fall toward the earth, that trees bend in the wind, that rivers flow downhill.

After many such walks, nature removed her veil, and my vision cleared. I suddenly understood how trees bending in the wind embodied the principle of *nonresistance*. Visualizing how gentle running water can cut through solid rock, I grasped the law of *accommodation*. Seeing how all living things thrived in moderate cycles, I was able to understand the principle of *balance*. Observing the regular passing of the seasons, each coming in its own time, taught me the natural order of life.

I came to understand that socialization had alienated me (and most adults) from the natural order, characterized by free, spontaneous expression; my young daughter, however, knew no separation from *things as they really are*.

Still, such insights seemed more poetical than practical, until, in a single moment, the final piece fell into place. I was taking a hot shower, enjoying the soothing spray, when my busy mind suddenly became quiet and I entered a reverie. The realization stunned me: *The laws of nature apply equally to the mind and the emotions.*

This may not seem like a big deal to you, but I dropped the soap. Grasping how nature's laws apply equally to the human psyche, itself inseparable from the body, made all the difference for me. The principles or processes of training were no longer merely physical. They became *psycho*physical. My perceptions even made a subtle shift: where once I viewed the world as a material realm, I now began to see a world of subtle forces and flowing energy, thus reaffirming our unbreakable connection to the laws of nature.

After fifteen years of gymnastics, my real training had finally begun. All that remained was to put this understanding to
use. As I did, the fruits of training began to spill over into daily
life. Training became a way of life, not just a means to an end.
And the game of athletics became a vehicle of body mind mastery — training for the game of life.

In describing the river of life, or the delicate, ephemeral existence of the butterfly, or the sway of trees in the wind, the
Chinese sages were painting pictures, drawing metaphors that
pointed to the natural laws, the source of all human wisdom.
Master teachers have each pointed to the same truth: that personal growth requires us to integrate the wisdom of life experience with the laws of nature.

Pursuing success in sport and life, I sought to align myself
with the following lessons and laws:

Principle 1: Nonresistance

There are four ways to approach the forces of life:

- Surrender to them fatalistically. Rocks, because they are
  inanimate, have little choice but to surrender passively to
  the natural laws.
- Ignore them and, in ignorance, experience accidents, or create unnecessary struggle by swimming against the natural
  currents of life.
- Resist them and create turmoil. If we resist what is — the
  natural flow of life — we waste energy and fight ourselves.
- Use them and blend with nature. Like birds that ride the
  wind, fish that swim with the current, or bamboo that
  bends to absorb the weight of fallen snow, you can make
  use of natural forces. This is the real meaning of nonresistance. We can express the law of nonresistance in many
  ways:

  - Don't push the river.
  - Let it be.

- Go with the flow.
- When life gives you lemons, make lemonade.
- Turn problems into opportunities and stumbling blocks into stepping-stones.

On days of slow physical progress, you can cultivate patience and trust in the natural process of growth. Nonresistance transcends passive acceptance and actively rides the currents and cycles, making use of whatever circumstances arise.

True nonresistance requires and develops sensitivity and wisdom. For the master, outer accomplishments are significant only as indicators of one's alignment with natural law. Master golfers, for example, make intuitive use of the wind, of the direction the grass grows, of the moisture in the air and the curves of the land. They use gravity by letting the weight of the club head guide the swing in a relaxed rhythm. Master gymnasts learn to blend with the forces and circumstances in their environment. Masters of tennis learn to use the texture of the court to their advantage.

In daily life, those of us who resist change inhibit growth. Bob Dylan reminded us that those who aren't busy being born are busy dying.

> *What a caterpillar calls the end of the world*
> *the master calls a butterfly.*
> *— Richard Bach*

A martial arts principle teaches, "If pushed, pull; if pulled, push." You can use your opponents' movements to your advantage through nonresistance. Apply softness in the face of hardness — absorbing, neutralizing, and redirecting force. Body mind masters reject the adversarial mindset; they cease perceiving and resisting "enemies." Rather, they view opponents as teachers or sparring partners who challenge them to bring out their best.

BLENDING

The Martial Arts Principle of No-Collision

Test 1. Stand squarely in front of a partner. Tense your body. Have the partner push you with one hand as you resist. How does that feel? What happens? You are likely to lose your balance or control as your partner pushes you backward.

The next time he or she pushes, take a smooth step back; just let your body flow backward at the same speed as your partner's push. Give no resistance at all. What does this feel like? Do you feel the cooperation and harmony you have created? Centered and in control, you allow your partner to go where he or she wants to go.

Test 2. Stand with your right leg and right arm extended toward your partner; root both your feet lightly to the floor. Breathe slowly in your lower abdomen; relax. Cultivate a feeling of peace and goodwill. As you maintain this spirit, have your partner come toward you rapidly from a distance of about ten feet, with the intent to grab your right arm, which is extended toward him or her at hip level.

Just as your partner is about to grab your hand, whirl around and behind your partner by taking a smooth, quick step slightly to the side and beyond your partner as he or she lunges past, grabbing for the arm that's no longer there. If you do this smoothly, facing your partner as you whirl around, you'll maintain equilibrium and control as your partner totters on the edge of balance.

Test 3. This Aikido approach can also be applied to potential verbal confrontations. On such occasions, instead of engaging in verbal tussling — trying to prove a point, win an argument, or overcome someone with reason — just sidestep the struggle. Simply listen, really listen, to your opponents' points; acknowledge the value of what they are saying. Then ask gently if there isn't some validity to your view also.

In this way, you can learn to blend and apply nonresistance not only to physical opponents but to all of life's little problems. Remember that you create the struggle in your life; you create the collisions. And *you* can dissolve conflict through nonresistance. ■

Nonresistance: Psychophysical Applications

In judo, he who thinks is immediately thrown.
Victory is assured to those who are
physically and mental nonresistant.
— Robert Linssen

Stress happens when the mind resists what is. Most of us tend to either push or resist the river of our lives, to fight circumstance rather than make use of things as they are. Resistance creates turbulence, which you feel as physical, mental, and emotional tension. Tension is a subtle pain, which — like any pain — signals that something is amiss. When we are out of natural balance, we create tension; by listening to our body, we can take responsibility for releasing it.

Athletes commonly resist the natural processes by *trying.* The word "try" itself implies weakness in the face of challenge. The moment you try, you are already tense; trying, therefore, is a primary cause of error. In more natural actions, you don't try. You simply walk to the refrigerator, write a letter, or water the flowers; you don't have to try, yet you perform these tasks easily and naturally. But when faced with something you consider an imposing challenge — when self-doubt arises — you begin to try. And when competitors feel pressure and begin to try, they often fall apart.

When archers shoot for enjoyment, they have all their skill;
when they shoot for a brass buckle, they get nervous;
when they shoot for a prize of gold, they begin to see two targets.
— Chuang Tzu

To illustrate the effect of trying too hard, imagine walking across a four-inch-wide plank of wood suspended a few inches off the ground. No problem, right? Now raise the plank ten feet over a pond filled with alligators. Suddenly you begin trying harder. You feel tense. You have the same plank but a different mental state.

Life is a play of polarities. Whenever you *try* to accomplish something, you often experience — and create — internal forces in direct opposition to your goal, just like those who *try* to lose weight but end up gorging. You can measure this opposition in your own physiology: if you *try* to hold your arm straight, you'll tend to tense your extensor muscles (triceps) but *also* your flexor muscles (biceps). You end up fighting yourself and wasting energy. If you *try* to stretch you may feel your muscles tensing in resistance, just as golfers who *try* to wallop the ball often end up topping it into the rough.

In all activities of life, the secret of efficiency
lies in an ability to combine two seemingly incompatible states:
a state of maximum activity and a state of maximum relaxation.
—Aldous Huxley

Body mind masters use less effort to create greater results. Even while engaged in intense competition they "let it happen" without strain. This may seem like idealistic fantasy, but num-

erous descriptions of the lives of martial arts masters testify to
the existence of this kind of grace under pressure. The higher
the stakes, the calmer, clearer, and more relaxed these masters
became — indeed they became unbeatable. Peaceful warriors
like Morehei Uyeshiba, the founder of Aikido, at more than
eighty years of age could evade an attacker wielding a razor-
sharp sword, tapping him on the nose with a fan, while remaining relaxed and breathing deeply.

Body mind masters take an easy, relaxed, progressive approach while working within the higher reaches of their comfort zone, thereby avoiding the burnout that accompanies a
stressful approach to training.

If you gently take a child by the hand and lead him or her
smoothly, the child is more likely to follow than if you give a
sudden tug. Our subconscious minds work the same way. In the
long run, it works better to use a carrot than a stick.

If you play golf, just *let* the club swing. If you're a gymnast,
form the intent, then *let* the body pirouette. If you play basketball, *let* the ball go through the hoop. In life, form clear goals,
prepare, then *let* things happen naturally, in their own good time.

Every bamboo shoot *knows* how to bend with the wind, but
masters have the insight to build windmills. Understanding the
spirit of nonresistance, you create a partnership with nature.
You take the first step on the path of body mind mastery.

Principle 2: Accommodation

Life was never meant to be a struggle,
just a gentle progression from one point to another,
much like walking through a valley on a sunny day.
— *Stuart Wilde*

Let's take a look at some key points in the process of learning:

- In athletics, as in life, development follows demand. With
  no demand, there is no development; with small demand,

small development; with improper demand, improper development.

- Demand takes the form of progressive overload. By persistently asking yourself to do more than you're comfortable with, slightly more than you are capable of, you improve.
- Progressive overload occurs in small increments within your comfort zone. You need to stretch your comfort zone but not ignore it. Most athletes constantly work outside their zone, and they experience extremes of fatigue, strain, and pain. By staying within (but near the top of) their comfort zone, masters take a little longer to improve, but their improvements last longer.
- Development inevitably entails a constant stream of "little failures" along the way to your ultimate goals.
- Tolerance for failure comes from an intuitive grasp of the natural process of learning. Realism breeds patience. By understanding natural laws, you develop a realistic, lighthearted approach to temporary failures and come to see them as stepping-stones to your inevitable progress.

When you make realistic and gradual demands on the body, the body will develop. If equally progressive demands are made on the mind and emotions, they will develop as well. This process of *accommodation* reflects a law that has allowed human beings to evolve and survive through time.

Even rocks are subject to the law of accommodation. If you grind a rock with a tool, it will gradually change its shape. But if you grind it too quickly, the rock may break. Gradual demand brings the surest results. Climbing a mountain is best done in small steps. If you try to do it in huge leaps, the result may be counterproductive.

The law of accommodation reminds us that mistakes are the stepping-stones to success — a natural part of the process.

Trust the process of your training and trust the process of your life.

Accommodation: Psychophysical Applications

Many of us are so goal-oriented that we forget to enjoy the journey. I'm reminded of an ancient Chinese curse: "May you achieve all your goals." Paradoxically, if we enjoy the process of striving toward our goals, we are more likely to reach them. Getting there is *more* than half the fun.

Accommodation is a law as certain as the law of gravity. Yet most of us don't trust the law because of self-doubt or confusion. You may wonder, "Can I really become good at this?" "Will I be able to accomplish my goal?" "Will I find success?" A more useful question is not "Can I?" but rather "*How* can I?" Progress is mechanical: If you practice something over time, with attention and commitment to improve, you will. The degree of improvement depends on many factors you'll discover as you read on. Some people have the unique combination of psychological, emotional, and genetic qualities necessary to become world-class, but *anyone* who practices over time can become competent, even expert, in any chosen endeavor.

PROOF OF ACCOMMODATION

Here's a simple way to understand how the law of accommodation works: Choose a physical action that is presently a little beyond your reach. It may be a push-up, a sit-up, a one-arm push-up, a handstand push-up, sitting on the floor with your legs straight out in front of you and touching your toes, or running in place for five minutes without tiring.

Once you've chosen your feat, attempt it several times in the morning and again in the evening. Do this every day. With each attempt, you're asking your body to change. Ask politely — don't overdo it — but be consistent.

Don't set any goals, time limits, or specific number of repetitions you must do each day. (Some days you may do more, other days, less.) Don't visualize any outcome.

Continue this for a month and see what happens. Without really trying, you'll find that somehow, in this relaxed way, you will have improved; your body will comply with your "polite request."

Apply the same approach to any change you'd like to make in your life. Achieving desired outcomes is a natural result of relaxed practice over time, of working within (but in the upper ranges) of your comfort zone, rather than pushing through pain. Trust the process; ask and it shall be given.

Of course, you may also benefit by setting, visualizing, even writing down specific goals. With no direction at all, you may wander in circles. So whether or not you affirm, visualize, or pursue other strategies, a goal in your mind and heart is a natural part of the process of accommodation. ∎

Applying the law of accommodation generates new levels of trust, responsibility, and commitment; your success depends on the demands you are willing to make on yourself. But know that when you decide to do something, even if it is not presently within your capacity, you can succeed. There are no absolute guarantees, but in making this journey you are more likely to succeed than if you never begin.

Principle 3: Balance

For the body mind master, balance goes far beyond a sense of equilibrium; it is a *great principle* informing every aspect of our training and our lives. I call it the Goldilocks principle: "Neither too much nor too little" — move neither too quickly nor too slowly, neither too actively nor too passively, neither too high nor too low, neither too far to one side nor to the other.

Balance determines the correct pace, timing, and accuracy we all depend upon for success in sport and life. The human body itself depends upon a delicate balance of blood chemistry and body temperature. It must breathe neither too quickly nor too slowly; it must develop into a unit neither too fat nor too lean, neither too muscular nor too emaciated. Even your intake of water and essential nutrients must be balanced. Everywhere you look, you can see the law of balance at work.

This law also recognizes our natural limitations. It is possible, of course, to go beyond the boundaries dictated by this law, just as you can temporarily resist the other natural laws, but eventually you pay an inevitable price because every action has a reaction, and the more extreme the action, the more extreme the reaction. When you are in balance, you recognize that for every *up* cycle there will naturally be a *down* cycle — and vice versa.

Progress in life generally consists of two steps forward and one step back. Some days are high energy days and others are not. Understanding this, your mind and emotions remain calm when training has its ups and downs, buoyed by the higher wisdom of the law of balance.

Balance: Psychophysical Applications

As it becomes more clear that the world — and your training — necessarily involves body, mind, and emotions, balance takes on even more profound significance. You begin to see that physical problems are often symptoms of imbalanced mental and emotional patterns. When you feel physically off, you should ask, "What's going on in my mind and emotions?"

The word *centered* describes a state of physical, mental, and emotional balance. The three centers — body, mind, and emotions — are so intimately connected that an imbalance in one naturally affects the others. The martial artist knows that if a person is mentally distracted or emotionally upset, he or she can be pushed over very easily.

The following tests demonstrate the uses — and abuses — of balance.

YOUR MIND-BODY BALANCE

Test 1. Assuming that you're relatively calm and happy right now, stand up and balance yourself on one leg. (If it's too easy, do it with your eyes closed.) Note the relative ease of this act.

The next time you feel upset — angry, sorrowful, fearful, or distracted, or are facing a difficulty in your life — give yourself the same balance test. You'll notice that one of two things will happen: If you meditate (focus attention) on your upset, you'll lose your balance easily. If you are meditate on your balance, you'll forget to notice your upset. Physical balance and emotional upset are like fire and water; they don't mix well.

Test 2. You can also gain control of an imbalance in body, mind, or emotions by deliberately doing something out of balance, in order to see the imbalance clearly and to control it.

To illustrate: The next time you practice any game, spend a few minutes deliberately off-balance, then back on balance, then off balance, then on. You will see your game begin to improve afterward. If you're too prone to imbalance in one direction, see if you can play too much in the opposite direction. If, for example, you're too timid in your play, try being too aggressive. If your tennis

serves veer too far to the right, make an effort to send
them too far to the left.

This practice will feel awkward, like wearing a suit
two sizes too small; nevertheless, it will do you a world of
good, because when you can play with both sides, you
can then find the middle and regain your balance. I
explain this invaluable method of attaining balance more
in Chapter 7. ■

Principle 4: Natural Order

Natural order accounts for progressive development through
time. In nature, one season follows another, without haste, in
the proper sequence. A tree grows from a seedling as an adult
grows from an infant.

Only the human being is in a hurry. Our minds race faster
than life. Ignoring the law of natural order, we set deadlines for
ourselves, rushing to reach these arbitrary goals. It's true we
must make *some* goals; they're essential for movement in life.
Without them, we wouldn't get out of bed in the morning. But
rigid *time* goals are inherently unrealistic, because we cannot
predict the future. The more long-range our goals, the less realistic they will be. We can foresee the *direction* of our progress,
but we cannot foresee the *pace*. Life holds too many surprising
twists and turns to accurately predict how much time our goals
will take.

Progress is a function of both time and intensity. You can
spend less time and more intensity, or more time and less intensity. If you overtrain, you may make more rapid progress and
even enjoy a short period of glory, but you eventually suffer
burnout.

Whatever cycles you pass through, trust in natural order.
Enjoy each day, come what may, with all your energy and

humor. Humor is a good sign that you have a balanced per-spective. After all, no matter how magnificent our athletic aspi-rations or achievements, we remain tiny specks in the great universe; missing a putt or double-faulting a serve is hardly going to shake up the cosmos.

Natural Order: Psychophysical Applications

Everyone at one time or another thinks, "I should be doing bet-ter — I should be achieving faster." Like the word "try," the word "should" has little place in the mind of the master. "Should" implies dissatisfaction with things as they are. It is the ultimate contradiction; it's the trembling foundation of neu-rosis. Our time is too valuable to spend stewing over things that are not.

One good measure of your alignment with the law of natur-al order is your level of enjoyment during the process of train-ing. If you push yourself too much, for too long, you may lose sight of the excitement that drew you to training in the first place.

So balance your life *between* pleasure and pain. Notice the natural order of things. Make use of whatever you meet on your path. Follow a step-by-step process, and trust what comes.

Working within natural law, you will not only find self-discovery and success, but you will enjoy life more with each passing year. Training mirrors life; life mirrors training. By examining one, you come to understand the other.

Alignment with natural laws provides the first key to suc-cess in sport and life. In the following chapters you can apply these principles to transcend limiting beliefs and behaviors, hurdle emotional blocks, and develop body mind talent — all steps in your journey up the mountain path.

CHAPTER TWO

The Power of Awareness

L ife is a *great school*, and nature is the ultimate teacher, but without awareness, or free attention, we miss life's teachings. Awareness transforms life experience into wisdom and confusion into clarity. Awareness is the beginning of all growth.

Learning is more than *knowing* something new; rather, it involves *doing* something new. The process of learning naturally involves errors. Masters make as many mistakes as anyone; but they learn from them. To correct and learn from an error, you need to become aware of it. *Awareness of a problem is the beginning of the solution.*

Body mind masters are willing to make fools of themselves, to accept their feelings of embarrassment or awkwardness, to begin anew and continue practicing.

The usual measure of progress in a sport is the results: if you win the match, sink the putt, accomplish your goal, then everything seems fine, but if you lose, you know *something* is wrong. Awareness transforms that vague "something" into a specific action you can correct or improve. As Lily Tomlin once said, "I always wanted to be somebody, but maybe I should have been more specific."

Most problems precisely defined are already partially solved.
— Harry Lorayne

If awareness were an intellectual capacity, then infants couldn't learn. But awareness extends far beyond conceptual understanding to a whole-body sensitivity arrived at through direct experience. Trying to learn or improve a skill without specific awareness is like trying to apply a postage stamp without adhesive — it won't stick.

> *Learn to think with the whole body.*
> — *Taisen Deshimaru, Swordmaster*

In training, as in life, errors are always with us. Learning is a process of refining errors to the point where they no longer prevent our desired goal. Errors exist even in our space program, but they have been minimized to an almost invisible level. Even the "perfect 10.0" routines of Olympic gymnasts contain errors, but they are small enough to be considered irrelevant.

Smaller errors make the master.

On our journey to mastery, become aware of weaknesses as well as strengths. Awareness of our weaknesses enables us to strengthen them and improve consistently. Awareness of our strengths breeds confidence and satisfaction.

Awareness, Disillusion, and Success

Awareness heals, but healing isn't always pleasant. Like a heavy drinker's first realization that "I am an alcoholic," awareness may be painful, but it frees us from illusion and empowers growth.

During my first few months training in the martial art of Aikido, I felt frustrated. Proper execution of the Aikido movements requires relaxation even while under attack. In the face of this demand to relax, I began to notice tension in my shoulders. At first I thought the training was *making* me tense. In fact, it seemed I was more tense than ever. But I came to realize that I was only becoming aware of tension I had always carried.

This awareness, while troubling, allowed me to see and move beyond my tension tendencies and to learn dynamic relaxation.

As my freshmen on the Stanford gymnastics team became more aware of their errors, they would tell me in frustration how they "used to be better in high school" and were "going downhill." This concerned me — until I saw films of them the year before, when it became obvious that they had improved radically. Now aware of their errors, they had raised their standards.

This feeling that you are "getting worse" is a sign of growing awareness. When writers are able to read their last draft and see their weaknesses, their writing progresses. Awareness in sport, in relationships, in any learning, often entails a momentary drop in self-esteem, a dent in self-image. But this willingness to clearly see and acknowledge our many mistakes — to doggedly but temporarily make a fool of ourselves — opens the door to body mind mastery. When we feel like we're "getting worse," we are finally ready to get much better.

Whole-Body Awareness

Most of us are willing to see our *physical* mistakes. The path of body mind mastery also entails the willingness to acknowledge our *mental* and *emotional* foibles — to see ourselves in a less flattering light. We all have shadow qualities, traits that are still immature or underdeveloped. These traits often remain hidden — especially from ourselves and our conscious awareness — only to surface momentarily in times of upset, pressure, or crisis.

We resist awareness of mental and emotional weaknesses because it's easier to see physical errors — you can visually observe the results. If you swing and miss the baseball, slice the golf shot, or serve into the net, for example, it's pretty obvious that you are making an error. Emotional and mental weaknesses are much more difficult to observe because the results of such weaknesses aren't as obvious or immediate.

We also identify more closely with our minds and emotions than we do with our bodies. Most people are more reluctant

to acknowledge mental or emotional illness than physical illness. It stings more when we're called stupid or immature than
when we're called physically awkward. What we identify with,
we tend to defend.

An ice-cream vendor, pushing his cart through a
park, stopped to listen to someone sermonizing. As the
speaker yelled, "Down with Fascism! . . . Down with
Communism . . . Down with big government!" he ice-
cream vendor nodded and smiled in agreement. But his
expression suddenly soured and he walked off, mutter-
ing under his breath, when the speaker added, "Down
with ice cream!"

Awareness is like sunlight over a dark well. You don't see
the creatures crawling around down there until the light of
awareness shines directly on them. This leads to humility, com-
passion, and freedom. Many of us, when faced with a relationship crisis or difficulty, have seen parts of ourselves we're not
too crazy about. The same kind of awareness emerges in the
fires of training and competition. After many years as an athlete and coach (and husband and father) I've had many opportunities to recognize my own foolishness. It's never easy on my
self-esteem, but these moments of insight and acceptance have
been essential to the progress I've made as an athlete and
human being.

> *Then the time came*
> *when the risk it took*
> *to remain tight in a bud*
> *was more painful than*
> *the risk it took to blossom.*
> *— Anaïs Nin*

For children, errors are natural; nearly all of what young
children do is make errors — learning to walk, drink from a
glass, or ride a bike. Kids wet their pants, fall over, drop things.

Yet they learn with a pace beyond nearly any adult. Once you drop your defenses and become "like little children" on your journey toward mastery, your learning accelerates.

Opening to the light of awareness provides a significant leap up the mountain path toward the peaks of body mind mastery.

The Growth of Awareness

Awareness, like everything else, is subject to the law of natural order, expanding from the gross (noticing you've just stubbed your toe) to the subtle (noticing that your energy and attention are out of balance). The following story illustrates the respect for refined awareness common in the East, especially in the martial arts traditions:

An old samurai warrior knew his time on earth was nearing an end and wished to bequeath his sword to the brightest of his three sons. He designed a test.

He asked a friend to hide just inside his barn, above the doorway, and gave him three small bags of rice. He then invited each son inside, one at a time.

The first son, after feeling the rice bag fall on his head, drew his sword and cut the bag in half before it hit the ground.

The second son halved the bag even before it hit his head.

The third son, sensing something amiss, declined to enter the barn — and so earned his father's sword.

> *I learned to speak as I learned to skate or cycle:*
> *by doggedly making a fool of myself until I got used to it.*
> — *George Bernard Shaw*

Beginners, by definition, are not yet aware of their errors in a particular skill. One sage reminds us, "We're all ignorant; only on different subjects." No matter what our accomplishments in certain areas of life, we're all beginners as we enter new territory.

The Margaret Analogy

At Oberlin College, I once had the pleasure of coaching a dedicated diver named Margaret. Her progressive growth of awareness in learning a particular dive parallels the stages we all go through in training — and in daily life.

After her first attempt at a dive, she had no awareness of what she had done wrong and had to rely entirely on my feedback.

After several attempts, she could recount what she had done incorrectly after the dive was finished and the errors had been made.

Before long she was becoming aware of her errors during the dive.

Finally, in one attempt, her awareness was integrated with body, mind, and emotions before the dive, and the errors were corrected before they were made. The dive was beautiful.

This example has profound implications for daily life, because we go through the same process in all kinds of learning situations. In athletics or in everyday life, self-awareness on all levels — physical, emotional, mental — must touch the core of your being, to the point of catalyzing a change in behavior. Intellectual awareness alone isn't enough.

Now comes a key point: Although we can *indirectly influence* our mind and emotions, we have little or no *direct control* over thoughts or feelings, which rise and pass like weather fronts. We have significantly more control over our behavior — despite what we are, or are not, thinking or feeling. In fact, our behavior (how we move our arms, legs, and mouth) is the only thing we can directly control. This is a great secret of success.

Feedback Aids to Awareness

When you know you're doing something wrong but don't know exactly what it is, use these awareness aids:

Other Students. The good and bad examples of those training with you can provide valuable lessons and models. Beginners remind you of your own progress. When you observe them improving as you did, you understand that you can also continue to improve. Advanced students serve as examples. Learning from example is the way infants learn — probably the most natural way to learn. Advanced athletes can inspire you by showing that high-level skills are possible.

Visual Feedback. Nothing serves the growth of awareness so instantly and so well as seeing a film or videotape of your own movements. Even a mirror can help you become realistic about your strengths and weaknesses.

The Coach. A videotape or film can show you what you look like, but only a teacher can pinpoint your specific errors in order of priority. A teacher is an intelligent feedback aid who can analyze and communicate information about errors and the ways to correct them. The coach or teacher who has journeyed farther up the mountain can show you how to avoid the pitfalls and overcome the hurdles.

Exaggeration. If you have no access to films or teachers or videotapes and want a shortcut to awareness, then deliberately exaggerate your errors. If you are slicing your golf ball or constantly falling in one direction, do it even worse — on purpose. In this way the error becomes clarified and your awareness expands. At the same time, your errors become conscious, deliberate, and controlled instead of unconscious — far easier to correct.

CHAPTER THREE

Preparation

If I had six hours to chop down a tree,
I'd spend the first four hours sharpening the axe.
— Abraham Lincoln

Preparation is to the athlete as the foundation is to a house. If you lack a solid foundation, you compromise the entire structure. Strong foundations are the first and most important step toward success in sport and life. A strong foundation is based upon complete preparation of body, mind, and emotions.

If you don't prepare fully, you risk developing bad or compensatory habits. Bad habits are like a tall tree or comfortable bed: easy to get into but hard to get out of. In fact, nearly every difficulty you face in your chosen training can be traced to skipping steps in the past — to a weakness in your foundation.

Champions form the habit of doing what most people find boring or uncomfortable. The secret of success is no secret at all — it comes down to sound preparation, a step-by-step process, and focused effort through the hurdles, peaks, and valleys. World-class and professional athletes regularly return to basics and strengthen their foundation. The reason most of us experience so many difficulties in our own training is that we were never taught to build a foundation based on mind and emotions — we just went straight to physical skills.

Few of us learned *how* to learn. The way most children learn athletics in school amounts to pure Darwinian survival of the fittest. The coach or teacher runs everyone through their paces and, in the end, the survivors make varsity; the others, who may learn more slowly, but learn well, are often left behind and may never discover their own potential.

As stated in the law of natural order, all things in nature have a gestation period and must undergo the proper stages in order to develop. Body mind mastery begins with profound preparation — the most difficult and important part of any learning process.

Ninety-five percent of making a vegetable stir-fry lies in the preparation: heating the wok to just the right temperature, cleaning and slicing the vegetables, making sure they are crisp. Then the cooking is easy. In painting a car, you must first go through the arduous work of cleaning the body, sanding it, filling in nicks, pounding out dents, sanding again, cleaning again, masking, priming — then, swish! The painting is easy. What would the paint job look like if you didn't prepare the auto properly first?

Physical skills are just the tip of the iceberg. The greater part — preparation — is invisible. Without this hidden foundation, the iceberg would topple. Creating success in sport and life is like building a house. The results are the visible part of the structure. Physical talent makes up the foundation of the house. Mental and emotional talent — internal qualities like clear focus and strong will — are the ground on which the house and foundation stand. No one drives by a house and says, "Wow! Will you look at that classy foundation!"

But without the foundation, the house will not stand.

A sage once said to me, "When in a hurry, take the long, sure way." There are no shortcuts up the mountain path. Say two spaceships race to Mars. One takes off earlier, but fails to prepare with sufficient fuel or provisions. The other ship remains, taking on a full supply of fuel. The first has a head start, but it's clear which will finish the journey.

Charting a Proper Course

The chart below illustrates three possible learning patterns.

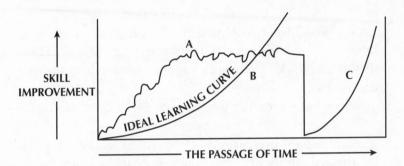

Curve A shows the hasty, random, up-and-down learning curve of most athletes. They improve rapidly at first, but as the skill requirements advance weaknesses begin to influence their performance more. Because of insufficient preparation — resulting from a weak foundation — the athletes' up-and-down cycles are amplified and progress eventually tapers off.

Curve B is the path of body mind masters. At first they appear to improve very slowly. The path is initially difficult, with little to show. These athletes are working "below the waterline," developing a hidden foundation. Gradually but surely, the learning curve begins to turn upward, until progress accelerates at a rapid, consistent, and almost effortless pace.

Curve C is really the most important, because it represents a second wind for most of us. If your preparation has been insufficient and you have been stuck on a plateau, you can duplicate the path of the natural athlete by first going back for a time — perhaps a few months — to do intense work on the "talent foundation" that will be explained fully in the following chapters on fundamentals. Allow yourself to progress slowly. In good time, your progress will accelerate again, and you will surpass your old marks.

In order to avoid falling onto path A, let's explore the primary reasons you might choose what may first seem a shortcut:

- You might not appreciate the importance of thorough preparation.
- You might not know what thorough preparation consists of.
- Lacking confidence, you may avoid frustration by going for immediate rewards (new skills) rather than carefully laying the groundwork of strength, suppleness, stamina, and fundamentals.
- You may have a teacher who follows the above thinking.

The immediate pressures of competition aggravate a tendency toward shortcuts, but master coaches continue to emphasis basics, fundamentals, and full preparation. When I coached the Stanford gymnastics team, the freshman had to endure a first year of going back to tune up their basics. They often felt frustrated because it seemed to them that their *progress* (learning new skills) was slowing down, and many felt they were getting worse (as their awareness of their weak fundamentals expanded). But by their second year, when they began to improve dramatically, they became believers in basics.

Beginning students cannot be expected to have a complete understanding of the training process and certain priorities within it. Therefore, an intelligent and patient coach is one of the most important aspects of your training. Choose with great care.

Step-by-Step Preparation

Whether you are concerned with physical, mental, or emotional preparation, a step-by-step approach to the task at hand can assure success. You may be attempting a complicated problem in physics; you may be job-hunting; you may be trying to perform a double-back somersault. Each of these tasks may seem difficult. But each can be broken down into a series of small steps that together represent a gradual, methodical process leading to the final goal.

Anything and everything in life can be broken down into its component parts. The more adept you become at the preliminary steps of preparation, the more you'll amaze yourself by what you accomplish. Then, when you focus on each of the intermediate steps, the process becomes more manageable and enjoyable.

Do what you can, with what you have, and where you are.

The Illusion of Difficulty

The term "difficulty" has meaning only in relation to preparation. If you've prepared well — if you've developed the physical, mental, and emotional qualities presented in this book — then learning skills comes easier. A well-prepared gymnast, for example, who has mastered a single somersault may actually find it *easier* to learn a double somersault than first learning the single somersault. Develop your talent foundation. Everything is difficult until it becomes easy.

The Coach as Master Teacher

Academic professors help train the mind, while coaches are responsible for developing the body, mind, and emotions of their students. Coaches also usually have a far more active, personal, hands-on responsibility for their students' progress and safety.

Coaches combine the attributes of a teacher, bio-technician, recruiter, motivator, organizer, fund-raiser, trainer, counselor, advisor, friend, role model, and sometimes sage. They invest in bodies, minds, spirits, and lives. The results of their efforts are publicly demonstrated at each and every game or event. They have a profound influence. They teach the laws of reality. They can help shape their students' character and lives.

The coach is your guide along the mountain path to achievement. Some guides are familiar with the lowlands; others can show you the entire way. The best guides know their own weaknesses and therefore have insight into yours; they can point out the obstacles but also the interesting side roads and beautiful scenery along the way. If your guide insists that you travel exactly the same path he or she did, then that guide's knowledge is limited. Seek a guide who can assess your qualities and point the best way for you. A teacher filled with natural awareness can light your way.

Second only to parents, teachers of movement can have a profound influence on a student's self-concept and outlook on life. Genuine movement teachers are able to convey useful lessons of living. Average teachers just teach skills. Beware of knowledgeable, skillful teachers who develop "winning" teams but at the same time smother the fundamental enjoyment and freedom of athletics.

Pick a teacher for yourself or your child with the same care you'd use to pick a surgeon. You wouldn't want a mediocre surgeon to operate on you — even if he or she was nice, had offices near your house, or charged a few dollars less. Yet this is how many people pick movement teachers. Finding a superior teacher for yourself or your child is worth some research and money, because an inspired teacher can have an influence that children will remember for the rest of their lives.

Teaching is an art of communication. If one teacher possesses 100 volts of knowledge but can effectively convey only 20 volts to his students, that teacher will be less effective than a teacher who combines 50 volts of knowledge with the ability to convey it all.

But do not be overawed by win-loss records or lists of advanced degrees. The important thing is not what *teachers* know but what their *students* know, not what teachers can do but what their students can do.

Good teachers speak the language of the intellect — words — and communicate clearly so that students understand. They use hindsight to learn by their mistakes and improve.

Excellent teachers speak the language of the body — by showing the muscles, bones, and nerves how an activity should feel if done properly. They use foresight to anticipate the consequences of their actions.

Great teachers speak the language of the emotions — by inspiring, motivating, and encouraging love of the sport. They use insight to access the wisdom of the ages.

Master teachers do all three, using sport as a means to teach life.

The Preparation of Children: A Note to Loving Parents

Children are likely to live up to
what you believe of them.
— Lady Bird Johnson

Considering the haste of today's schedule-obsessed world, our tendency to hurry now and then is understandable. But our haste to achieve spills over onto our children, and this is *most* apparent in children's athletics. Soon we may see Diaper League Championships, complete with preschool cheerleaders and over-achieving parents. Instead, however, I would recommend the following:

Movement play for young children — even infants — provides their vital little bodies with exercise, stimulation, and a means of discovering their relationship to the natural laws. The skill level they achieve is less important than learning:

- to feel good about their bodies
- to experience success early on by beginning with relatively easy tasks
- to enjoy active movement through accomplishment
- to develop confidence by completing tasks

We should measure success not by parental goals but by a child's beaming smile. Children should play with other children, on child-sized equipment in a child-sized environment of color, softness, and safety. Early injuries, fears, or failures can affect children far into the future.

I don't usually recommend private lessons — especially if Mom or Dad is the prospective teacher. A well-intentioned adult may give patient and skilled instruction, but children often perceive in a private tutor a larger, infinitely more capable role model they cannot hope to emulate successfully. This can be very discouraging. (On the other hand, watch how children delight in seeing Mom or Dad fumble, and how they laugh with glee when you let them feel stronger or smarter than you.) A good learning environment for a child is within a small group of other children, some more skilled and some less so.

Early play can help prepare a child for easier development later on, but the focus should remain on early play that feels good and not on intense training. It is also best to avoid early competitive emphasis.

Children can begin different kinds of movement training at different ages. The main factors determining when to start are the development of the bones and joints, the attention span, and natural interest. If your children are interested in an activity, let them try it, whether you are interested or not, if they are willing to commit at least three months to it. If you push a child into an activity that interests only you, be prepared for eventual disappointment.

If your children are motivated and well prepared, it will take only about four or five years of serious training to approach their highest level of achievement. The later years of training bring only subtle refinements and will not stabilize their attainments. You don't need, therefore, to start "budding Olympians" in long workouts before they are out of diapers.

Overinvolved parents who, in their loving enthusiasm, want to help their youngsters too much often do more harm than good. Too much parental interest can confuse children and weaken their motivation. They are never sure whether they are participating to please themselves or just their parents. Children under parental pressure will feel this internal contradiction no matter how their parents assure them. Children can be acutely sensitive to parental aspirations — far more than it appears — and will quickly see through your lie to the fantasy behind it.

What you can offer your children is emotional and financial support, transportation to classes, and confidence in their learning process. It's great to attend an occasional game, but overzealousness or wild excitement when your children win may make them feel that you're equally disappointed in them when they lose.

Whether or not your children are naturally inclined to active sports, or music, or martial arts, or dance, they can benefit from a regular form of training — of the body, mind, and emotions. There is something for every child; it is for them and their parents to discover what fits the children's personalities.

> *Treat children as though they are already the people*
> *they are capable of becoming.*
> *— Haim Ginott*

Sound preparation and the magic of time helps both adults and children to realize their fullest potential.

PART TWO

Developing Talent

Everyone has a talent; but rare is the courage to follow the talent to the places it leads.
— Erica Jong

Every time I teach at a sports camp I observe gymnasts and other athletes who practice diligently but meet obstacles because they haven't yet developed the key qualities of talent that could help them learn skills faster, easier, and at a higher level.

We all know that chains break at their weakest link. Yet athletes — or businesspeople or teachers — may avoid spending sufficient time working on their weak links. Because we like to feel successful, we tend to spend more time demonstrating our strong points than struggling through the less pleasant, and more arduous, work of shoring up our weaknesses.

We often let strength in one sphere compensate for weakness in another — making up for lack of flexibility with strength, for example. By emphasizing fundamental talent drills early in your career you can build a well-rounded foundation of talent.

Developing a balanced foundation can save time, prevent injury, and create talent for sport and life. As a high school freshman, Tom Weeden decided that he wanted to become one of the nation's premier gymnasts — not an unusual goal for

many young athletes. What was unusual was that Tom method-
ically sought advice from every coach he could find. As one of
those coaches, I suggested that he begin by developing strength,
suppleness, and correct fundamentals before he concentrated
on fancy skills — advice I had shared with many young athletes. But Tom had the patience and wisdom to actually follow
this advice. While other gymnasts were making a name for
themselves, Tom worked quietly and diligently on his talent
foundation. Then, about a year later, he suddenly began winning every competition he entered. First he won local events,
then regional, then national — until Tom Weeden made the
United States Olympic Team.

No matter what your limitations, no matter how your body
looks or feels — even if you've been in a slump for a year — if
you're willing to undergo the initiation necessary to develop
your talent, you will become a body mind master. All the qualities are within you. You may have to direct more energy and
time than someone else does in order to bring out the right
qualities, but you absolutely have the capacity to do it.

> *An overnight success usually takes about ten years.*
> — *Anonymous*

The next three chapters provide a map of the talent process,
beginning with the master key: the mind.

CHAPTER FOUR

Mental Talent

The mind leads the body.
— Koichi Tohei

Golf is twenty percent technique and eighty percent mental.
— Ben Hogan

Have you ever been lost in thought while someone was talking to you, when you suddenly realized you hadn't heard a thing they were saying? Or maybe you've driven through a stop sign without seeing it? Your ears and eyes were open, but your attention was captured by random thoughts or daydreams. Attention moves in two fundamental directions — outward, to the world of energy and movement, or inward, to thoughts. For most of us, attention bounces randomly back and forth between the inner and outer worlds.

Psychotics are an extreme example of people completely lost in thought — turning their attention inward is so compelling that they lose contact with external reality. Most of us are subject to the same tendencies, but to a lesser degree, as our attention drifts from the present to the past or the future.

If you sit down in a quiet room and close your eyes, you'll notice many subliminal thoughts that usually play just below the threshold of your conscious recognition. As you sit quietly you may also become aware of the rhythmic expansion and release of your breath. You may notice the beating of your heart and, eventually, more subtle internal displays of sound

and light. Above all, you'll notice the stream of thought, flowing on and on.

Most of us are subject to patterns of fuzzy attention, floating back and forth, in and out — a parade of reveries, fan-
tasies, concerns, plans, problems, fears, anger, expectations,
sorrows, regrets, and rehearsals. Emotionally charged thoughts
often command our attention. Pay attention and test this truth
in your own experience.

> *How can you think and hit at the same time?*
> *— Yogi Berra*

Meditation practice — whether sitting, standing, or moving
— develops insight into the process of your thoughts. By paying
attention in this way, you are able to recognize, acknowledge,
and accept thoughts and feelings, but no longer let them drive
your behavior or run your life. This is the beginning of body
mind mastery. The first step to transcending the mind is to
notice how you blame external circumstances for your anger —
to understand that the problem lies not simply in the circumstance but in your mind's resistance to *what is.*

> *I've had many troubles in my life,*
> *most of which never happened.*
> *— Mark Twain*

Body mind masters have learned in sport and life to focus
their attention on the present moment — the next pitch, the
next shot, the next swing — or washing the dishes. Thoughts
come and go, but the body mind master's attention remains
focused on the here and now. You can apply this skill to the
practice of daily life. This *practice of the present moment* may
be one of the greatest benefits of any form of training.

REALITY CHECK

Take this amusing test: A door swings open before you, and you see a sink full of water. The drain is plugged, and the water is running. The water begins to pour over the sink's edge. Do you turn off the water and pull the plug, or do you grab a mop?

Many athletes, and others facing the problems of daily life, spend a lot of time "mopping up" — dealing with symptoms. Many couples, for example, argue constantly about various topics when they need to focus instead on communicating more effectively. Developing mental talent involves "pulling the plug" on the primary source of emotional turbulence and physical tension.

One way to appreciate your present state of mind is to contrast it with that of a typical three-month-old. Babies store many of the impressions of movement and energy they perceive in the world. But because they can't talk, and because they don't yet have complex associations, beliefs, opinions, values, and attitudes relative to those impressions, they don't think much *about* anything. Children don't philosophize, conceptualize, or theorize. Their attention is entirely focused in the present moment, without judgment or expectation. While their intellects are undeveloped, their attention is also free of the complex fears, angers, attachments, expectations, plans, biases, self-imagery, and self-criticism that characterize most adult minds. Such "ignorance" is bliss.

Babies are body mind masters in their clarity, relaxation, sensitivity, and openness to the environment, and in their simple, direct approach to life — free of mental reaction and resistance. These qualities account not only for their astounding learning abilities but also for their innate charm and spontaneity.

When you pay close attention to what you are doing, your mind quiets; and in that moment of silence, the symphony begins. ∎

We all began life as movement masters, our minds free of meaning. When a child learns to stand and walk, they fall down a lot. But they don't judge their performance or compare themselves to anyone else — "I'm such a klutz! I'll bet the baby across the street could walk circles around me!"

A first step in reclaiming our innate potential is to examine four obstructions that plague most of us: limited self-concept, fear of failure, destructive self-criticism, and lack of concentrated attention. The following sections deal with these key mental obstructions.

Limited Self-Concept

> *Those who believe they can*
> *and those who believe they can't*
> *are both right.*
> *— Henry Ford*

Your progress in life tends to consistently follow your expectations. This is often called the self-fulfilling prophecy, and it applies to any field of endeavor. If you expect to do poorly, you will be less motivated and less interested; you'll commit less time and energy and thus won't perform as well, which only reinforces your limiting belief. If you expect or believe that you are a great dancer, or that you aren't very likable, or that you are a whiz at math, you set in motion behaviors and choices that will fulfill your expectations.

Thus, in sport and life, your level of achievement tends to mirror your self-concept. An example is the story of the self-limiting shoe salesman who was given a one-hundred-square-mile area in which to sell shoes. The first month he generated $10,000 worth of business. His supervisor was so pleased that he doubled the salesman's territory the next month. Nevertheless, the salesman still sold only $10,000 worth of shoes. Upset, the supervisor cut his area to half its original size. That month the salesman still sold $10,000 worth of shoes. He had a $10,000-a-month self-concept.

When you were very young, you were free to learn — ready for anything. As you grew, however, you began to receive signals that you were good at some things and bad at others. You were praised and blamed, or lacked experience, or misunderstood the situation, as I did when I was five, when I started kindergarten three weeks after my classmates.

In painting class, I made my first picture of a tree. It looked like a green lollipop, since it was my first try. Then I looked around at the paintings of the other children, and to my disappointment, their paintings looked like trees. I didn't understand that they had practiced drawing many more trees than I had. I didn't realize that, if I continued to practice as much as they had, my trees might look even more leafy than theirs. But I gave up too soon. Then and there, I decided that I was not a good painter.

Three-year-old Sam formed a self-concept another way. Reaching for a glass of milk, he misjudged the distance and knocked the milk over. His mother, momentarily upset, exclaimed, "Oh, clumsy child!" This word "clumsy" was new to him. He figured it had something to do with milk.

On another occasion, it happened again — but this time, with juice. "Clumsy!"

"Ah," Sam reasoned. "It doesn't mean milk, it means spilling that makes me clumsy." Soon he had several dozen glasses of spilled liquid and a few falls down flights of stairs to prove it.

As a child, you were pure potential. You could learn anything within human capacity. You had within you the seeds of becoming a physician, an attorney, an engineer, a craftsman, a dancer, an artist, or an Olympian. It never occurred to you that learning was difficult. You were free from assumed limitation, like my friend Jim Fadiman's daughter in a story he told me:

> My four-year-old daughter decided that she wanted to learn to fly. It seemed elementary enough to her — even birds could do it. She stood on the couch and jumped, her arms flapping. Her first attempt was not entirely successful.
>
> She reasoned that since birds have feathers, this must be the missing ingredient. She found a feather in the yard. Holding it in her little hand, she leaped again into the air. She told me that the feather had "definitely helped."

In letting his daughter jump from the couch, Jim was allowing her to safely explore her natural powers and limitations. In this way she was able to gain a balanced, realistic view of her abilities, uncolored by other people's expectations. When I asked Jim why he hadn't just saved her some effort and explained to her that little children can't fly, he replied, smiling, "How could I know? I might have been wrong."

Whenever older children or adults began one of my gymnastics classes, I could see them acting out roles based on their self-concept. A few people play the role of class leaders, get in front of the line, and show what they can do. Others stand quietly at the end of the line, making remarks like, "Oh, I'm really not coordinated."

Your self-concept relates to your activities in daily life. You may have a fairly high self-concept in athletics but a lower one in auto mechanics, bookkeeping, painting, writing, or connecting VCRs to TVs.

Self-concept is no more real than the shadow of a shadow. It is an illusion imposed on you long ago. Yet this illusion can limit your every endeavor until you can see it for what it is and cut through it. You transcend self-concept through understanding — by seeing through it — opening your talent for body mind mastery.

> *In order to achieve all that is demanded of us*
> *we must regard ourselves as greater than we are.*
> — *Johann Wolfgang von Goethe*

A WISH LIST

One way to overcome limiting self-concepts is to write down a list of twenty qualities or abilities you possess, or activities you might like if you felt you could do them well. Once the list is complete, rate yourself on a scale from one to ten — one being totally inept and ten being world-class. Don't limit yourself to writing down only those activities you actually perform; include activities you tend to avoid.

Once you've rated yourself, examine this reflection of your self-concept. Pay particular attention to your low self-ratings. Do you enjoy any of the activities? Why or why not? Have you ever really put effort into these activities in order to become proficient? Are there any authentic reasons you couldn't become good at these skills? People with no arms have become excellent painters; I've seen a one-legged man become a fine springboard diver; blind people have excelled at running marathons and bouncing on the trampoline. What's your excuse?

Here's the final step in this exercise: When you finish this chapter, sit quietly and consider these points about illusory self-concept. Look over your list one more time. Then burn it. ■

Through the insight that self-concepts are often illusory, you can overcome self-imposed limitations. That's when your training builds new momentum.

Sometimes . . . you feel that you can do anything.
At times like this I can run up to the front of the board,
stand on the nose pushing out through a broken wave;
I can put myself in an impossible position
and then pull out of it.
— Midget Farrelly, champion surfer

The danger of low self-concepts may seem obvious, since they limit your achievement. But unrealistically high self-concepts have their own unique problems. Young children who are constantly praised for everything get used to such praise, which represents the positive attention that all children crave. They will strive to maintain this praise and maybe even develop precocious abilities.

The shadow side is that their self-esteem depends at first on the praise and is transferred later to the achievement that earned the praise. They grow up to expect success, and they project this expectation onto other people, so that everyone in the world expects them to succeed. This expectation becomes a tremendous pressure not to let the world down. It can create brilliant students, star athletes, and suicides.

Unrealistically high *or* low self-concepts create problems. The best self-concept is none at all. Children raised in a home relatively free from exaggerated praise or blame form a realistic, experimental, and persevering approach to their pursuits, without undue psychic pressure. They explore life and achieve out of a natural and innate sense of curiosity and internal satisfaction rather than external stroking or reward. They achieve naturally and enjoyably, without undue stress, in their own good time.

Competence breeds confidence. So pay attention to each small success. Pat yourself on the back more and kick yourself less. Above all, keep training. Michael Jordan didn't sink every free-throw, but he did take the shot. And by constantly taking shots in your life, you increase your chances of success.

Start making positive, rather than the usual negative, statements about your worth, your potential, your skill — whether or not you fully believe them. With every positive statement to yourself — "I am an accurate putter," "I perform well under pressure," "I remember names and faces," "I enjoy not smoking" — you open doors to new possibilities.

Visualize your dreams in detail. Your subconscious mind doesn't clearly differentiate between what you visualize in your mind's eye and what you see with your physical eye, so the more you visualize positive outcomes, the more you attract them to your life. When I was competing in gymnastics I spent a lot of time visualizing myself performing fantastic routines; I believe this habit accounted for much of my success.

Success breeds success because it undermines assumed limitations. And remember that the natural law of accommodation is stronger than any self-concept. If you practice over time, you *will* improve. Transcending self-concept is a primary step on the path of the body mind master.

Fear of Failure

I used to fail at least fifty times a day in the gym. Failure is a natural part of the learning process — a signpost and guide to progress. In order to learn, you have to examine what's not working and change your behavior accordingly. One successful

CEO of a Fortune 500 company said that if he could live his life over, he would "make more mistakes and learn from them."

Most of us were taught as children to fear failure — especially public failure — and to avoid it at all cost. No one wants to be called a *loser*. So you learn defense mechanisms like "not really trying." By clinging to the belief that "I could have done it if I'd really tried, but it wasn't important enough to me," you never *really* fail.

Fear of failure produces tension; tension constricts the blood flow and slows the reflexes, which produces shallow breathing; shallow breathing results in the contraction of opposing muscle groups, which reduces coordination. Ultimately, fear of failure generates a vicious circle that creates what is most feared.

To break this cycle, you need to make peace with failure. It isn't enough merely to tolerate it; you need to appreciate failure and use of it. Allow a half-dozen errors each game — even miss on purpose once in a while — just to stay loose and keep a balanced perspective. If we can make ourselves miss, we can also make ourselves hit.

Body mind masters have made peace with failure, treating it like an old friend playing a practical joke. The greatest inventors, artists, and athletes all failed many times. Babe Ruth was the home run king of his time, but also the strikeout king.

Destructive Self-Criticism

There are two kinds of criticism in the world:

1. Constructive: "You were a little too high on that one; try swinging lower on the next."
2. Destructive: "That's all wrong! Boy, that was dumb!"

If babies held the same tendency toward self-criticism as adults, they might never learn to walk or talk. Can you imagine infants stomping the floor and screaming, "Aarggh! Screwed up again!" Fortunately, babies are free of self-criticism. They just keep practicing.

Self-criticism is a learned habit pattern, one that usually begins in childhood, when children naturally make errors and often receive destructive criticism.

If you received destructive criticism as a child, you later internalized that criticism and began to criticize yourself to prevent others from doing so. This childhood defense usually *does* tend to deflect criticism from parents, brothers, sisters, or playmates, but it's a hard habit to break.

Some believe that we have to criticize ourselves to improve. Just the opposite is true. The judgment only holds the pattern in place.

So be gentle with yourself; show yourself the same kindness and patience you might show a young child — the child you once were. If *you* won't be your own friend, who will be? If, when playing an opponent, you are also opposing yourself, you will be outnumbered.

You probably would find it cruel and unnecessary to say to someone, "You are really stupid; you keep making the same mistakes; you should give up; you'll never be any good!" Yet we think it's okay to say the same things to ourselves.

> *Others will underestimate us,*
> *for although we judge ourselves*
> *by what we feel capable of doing,*
> *others judge us only by*
> *what we have already done.*
> — *Henry Wadsworth Longfellow*

One-Pointed Attention

There is tremendous power in total attention to the matter at hand. In the intensity of performance or competition we are more likely to focus our minds on the present moment, forgetting all else, than when performing habitual routines such as driving, walking, or eating, when we tend to daydream. But athletes in action experience the power of the present moment. And in these moments of truth, we can find silence and serenity.

When we achieve one-pointed attention, we become completely present. This state has been called *flow* or being *in the zone*. The body mind master calls it *home*.

When I play my best golf, I feel as if I'm . . . standing back
watching the earth in orbit with a golf club in my hands.
— Mickey Wright

When skiers and surfers feel this total attention, they *know* they won't fall. Golfers in this state can sense lines of energy from the ball to the hole. Tennis players in the zone anticipate what is going to happen before it happens.

As you learn to attain one-pointed attention to the present moment, you lift the quality of your sport and life.

You ignore everything and just concentrate.
You forget about the rest of the world and become part of
the car and the track. It's a very special feeling. You're
completely out of this world and completely into it.
There's nothing like it.
— Jochen Rindt

MIND AND BODY

The following exercise shows how even a subtle distraction affects the body: Ask a friend to stand comfortably with his arms at his sides. Ask him to tense one arm, locking it straight and clenching his fist, with his arm pointed downward along the side of his body. Tell him you are going to try to pull his arm away from his body, sideways, a foot or two. Notice the amount of effort required for you to pull the arm out.

Next, tell him that you are going to wave your hand in front of him, with a zigzag motion downward, without touching him, and then you'll immediately try again to pull his arm out as you did the first time. Proceed to do this.

Do you notice the difference? What happened to his mental focus when you distracted him with your hand? ■

*Obstacles are those frightful things you see
when you take your eyes off the goal.*
— *Hanah More*

Athletic training is the best school for one-pointed concentration because it demands your full attention in the present. Body mind masters develop the ability to follow through in sport or life, no matter what distractions assail them.

*I wasn't worried about a perfect game going into
the ninth. It was like a dream. I never thought
about it the whole time. If I'd thought about it
I wouldn't have thrown a perfect game.*
— *Catfish Hunter*

A gymnast's *mind* falls off the beam before her body does. In order for her to maintain perfect balance, she must keep her attention squarely over the beam. As the saying goes, *"Don't look where you don't want to go."* Before a football running back can be tackled, he must be distracted. Becoming unstoppable depends more on mental focus than physical skill.

The following two-part exercise can show you the difference between weak attention and total one-pointedness:

> **Test 1.** Stand and squarely face a partner from a distance of about ten feet. His feet should be a shoulder-width apart, each the same distance from you. Now, assuming a timid stance, walk in a straight line, as if to brush past his right side. As you are about to pass him, have him lift his right arm directly in front of your chest. Let your mind stop at the arm in front of you.
>
> **Test 2.** This time, perform exactly the same exercise, with one mental difference. Walking the same speed, project your attention, with force, a thousand miles in front of you. Pay no attention to your partner's arm as it is raised; continue right through the arm as if it weren't there. Remain relaxed, positive, centered. What do you experience?
>
> Your partner's arm represents those little distractions of daily life, the thoughts that spring up to distract you. Fear and distractions will continue to arise. But when you pay as little attention to them as you did your partner's arm, you'll be on your way to one-pointed attention and body mind mastery. ∎

Every basketball player has experienced the difference between shooting a basket with full attention and attempting the same with only partial concentration. If, for example, Stretch is about to shoot with his attention divided between the basket and the opponent guard behind him, he'll likely miss a shot he could easily make in practice. Experiment on your own with Trash Basketball:

TRASH BASKETBALL

Sit about 10 feet away from a wastebasket. Crumple some waste paper into about twenty little balls. Get ready to play.

Step 1. Without paying real attention, casually toss some balls toward the basket, and see if you sink any.

Step 2. This time, focus your attention intently in the center of the wastebasket. Sink your mind into the basket. Staying relaxed, toss a few balls in. (Remember not to *try* or you'll become tense; just let them go in.) Check your results. Were you focused?

Step 3. Repeat Step 2, but have a partner standing behind you periodically poke you in the ribs, at random, as you're about to shoot. Notice how this affects your mental focus and accuracy. Then overcome it. ∎

One-pointed attention brings freedom from internal distractions and can help you master any game. Such mental power carries over into the games of life. As you stabilize your ability to focus your attention fully on the matter at hand, you will find yourself resting more and more in the present moment. Life will become more simple, profound, and full.

Freedom from mental distraction equals power. Olympic champion weightlifters not only have powerful bodies; they have powerful minds. The same quality of attention frees us, in the moment of truth, from any thought of self-concept, criticism, or fear. Body mind masters eventually come to the realization that this and every moment, on or off the field, is the moment of truth.

We have to isolate mental qualities before we develop them. Training is either conscious and systematic, or random and haphazard. If you feel something wrong with your running as you jog around a track but aren't able to pinpoint the specific problem, you'll struggle to improve by doing more of the same. But as you learned in Chapter Two: The Power of Awareness, you need to clarify a problem before you can solve it.

> *You're involved in the action and vaguely aware of it —*
> *your focus is not on the commotion but on the opportunity*
> *ahead. I'd liken it to a sense of reverie . . . the insulated state*
> *a musician achieves in a great performance . . . not just*
> *mechanical, not only spiritual; something of both,*
> *on a different plane and a more remote one.*
> *— Arnold Palmer*

Golfers experience periods when they can't seem to sink a putt; tennis players often have double-fault slumps. Because they can't identify the source of their problem, these athletes may look to the heavens, wondering why the gods are punishing them. They start carrying rabbit's feet wrapped in garlands of four-leaf clovers. They develop nervous tics or superstitious rituals. They may even voluntarily commit themselves to rest homes.

Now that you have a better understanding of the mental mechanisms that influence your performance, you'll realize that although we all find ourselves in slumps occasionally, we don't need to get stuck in them. And when you feel like you're going nowhere or even slipping backward, you may actually be backing up to get a running start.

So when the time comes to act, remember to lose your mind and come to your senses. Now we'll turn to the realm of emotions — the fuel for your journey.

CHAPTER FIVE

Emotional Talent

Nothing great was ever achieved without enthusiasm.
— *Ralph Waldo Emerson*

You may understand and have a sound vehicle for the journey, but whether your journey travels through athletics or daily life, you need sufficient fuel to get moving.

Different from physical energy, emotional energy creates the critical impulse to move you toward your goals — often called motivation. When emotional energy flows through us freely, without obstructions, we feel naturally motivated. And no force is more powerful than a motivated human being. We've all heard success stories about underdogs who produced miracles through powerful motivation. Motivation serves as a key to any training and beats at the heart of emotional talent.

Inspiration and motivation can be the difference between victory and defeat, success and failure, even life and death. The energy derived from motivation carries distance runners past the "wall of pain" when their physical energy reserves are exhausted. On the other hand, strapping athletes bursting with vital physical energy who lack direction may wander aimlessly and arrive nowhere in particular.

But motivation, like all emotional states, comes and goes, rises and falls. I certainly didn't feel motivated all the time during my gymnastics career. But I trained six days a week, for more than four hours a day, for years, by keeping my eye on the goal. Although motivation comes and goes, you can always rely on your will. Still, motivation is like an umbrella on a rainy day. You can go out without it — by applying your will — but it makes for a more enjoyable journey.

Once released, the power will transcend our changing emotions. An obstacle is just something we worry about when we've taken your eyes off the goal.

I've seen athletes with real physical limitations develop into national champions through directed emotional energy. Eric Courchesne, a teammate of mine, had had polio as a child. His legs were so atrophied that when I first met him he required braces or crutches to walk. He became a specialist on the rings. He simply worked harder than anyone. He not only developed superior strength, he also began to practice a dismount from the rings that took him about nine feet in the air. He performed a full-twisting somersault and, by some incredible feat of will, landed unassisted on his weakened legs. Over and over I'd see him crash to the floor. His brother told me he used to go home and cry, the pain in his legs was so intense. After three years, Eric was able to run around the gym without leg braces. He tied for first place in the national championships.

Life demands much of us, on and off the playing field. Emotional talent is the capacity to stimulate and draw upon our natural fountain of energy — to learn to blow into our own sails. We develop emotional talent not by relying on motivation all the time but by applying our will no matter how we feel.

As a baby, motivation was natural to you — everything was interesting. On occasion you tensed your little body and cried, but crying was a simple, natural response to physical discomfort, rather than mental worries. Your mind was free of thought — in a state of clarity, focus, and attention. Your body was free of tension — sensitive, and conducting the energies of life. You naturally felt this state of pure energy and motivation. Nothing impeded this fuel for action — the impulse to move, to explore, to grow.

As you grew and became more aware of rules, meanings, associations, interpretations, right and wrong, success and failure, and all the other demands of the world, you began to separate from the protected cradle of infancy. Vulnerable to a world of emotional turbulence, social turmoil, and human frustration, you began to know guilt, doubt, and anxiety.

Body mind masters do not deny or repress their feelings but learn to stay physically relaxed even under stressful conditions. Even when feeling angry, fearful, and sorrowful, breathe evenly and fully. Keep your body relaxed. You have much more control over your behavior than you do over your thoughts or emotions, so paradoxically the best way to master your emotions is to let them be, stay relaxed, and focus on constructive action. So, accept your emotions as natural to you in the moment, without trying to fix them. Know your purpose or goal — not someone else's. And, do whatever you need to reach that goal, whether or not your emotions or moods help or hinder you. These are three principles that carry well into daily life.

Breaking the Circuit of Tension

The mind imposes tension on the body and is one source of emotional turmoil. But until you master the mind, how do you break the harmful circuit of stress?

Follow this technique to regain emotional equanimity:

TENSE, SHAKE, BREATHE, AND RELAX

- Deliberately tense your whole body as tightly as you can for three to five seconds, while holding your breath.
- Then gently shake your body.
- Next, stand tall, as if your head were suspended in space from a string, and breathe slowly, deeply, and

evenly from your lower belly. Let the breath bring a
sense of deep relaxation.

Undoing emotional habits formed over the years
isn't easy, but you can do it. In any moment, you have
the capacity to breathe deeply, relax, and let go. Allow
rather than resist what arises in the present moment —
inside or out. Let it be interesting rather than *good* or
bad. In this way, you reawaken true emotion and the
energy to act. ■

Breath and Feeling

Inspiration, in addition to its usual definition, also means to
breathe in. The breath is a key to your emotional state because
it both reflects and affects your level of tension. Learning to
breathe with full feeling gives you the ability to *inspire* yourself.

The breath is a unifying link between mind and body.
Meditation works with the mind but also relaxes the body.
Relaxation exercises, in turn, work with the body but also
affect the mind. Both body and mind are intimately related to
the emotions through awareness of the breath. Various
approaches to well-being demonstrate the intimate relationship
of the three centers: physical, mental, and emotional.

Meditation practices center around insight and release of
thought. As thoughts pass, emotions flow naturally, and the
body relaxes. And as you relax your body, you consciously
release emotion-producing tension — another step on the path
of body mind mastery.

Ultimately, we gain mastery over emotions by controlling
the body. And a good place to begin is to observe and control
your breathing. Yogis, Zen masters, and martial artists have all
placed great emphasis on proper breathing. Such awareness
and discipline are central to the teachings of the most ancient

spiritual traditions. The body mind master, like the infant, breathes naturally from deep in the belly, with slow, full, relaxed, and balanced inhalations and exhalations.

If you observe your and others' breathing over a long period of time, you will see that the three primary emotional obstructions — anger, sorrow, and fear — are each linked with an imbalance in breathing.

Anger is reflected by weak inhalation and forceful, exaggerated exhalation.

Sobbing, a physical expression of sorrow, is characterized by spasmodic, fitful inhalation and weak exhalation.

Fear can result in very little breathing at all. As you consciously develop awareness of your breathing patterns, you can recognize these reactive patterns and use the breath as a key method of balancing body, mind, and emotions.

The following exercise will give you a feeling for proper breathing and its effect on the body:

BREATHING

Sit comfortably, on a chair or cushion. Your spine should be upright but not stiff.

Tension breathing. For a few minutes, breathe with your shoulders raised upward. Breathe using the upper chest only; take shallow breaths. Experience how this feels.

Natural breathing. Relax the shoulders by lifting and dropping them a few times, until they just hang. Feel their weight. Keep the mouth closed, the chin tucked gently in, and the eyes closed. Breathe slowly and deeply, but without any sense of strain. When you inhale, feel your belly draw downward and slightly outward. When you exhale, let the belly relax back up and in. Do this for at least ten minutes, remembering to relax your shoulders, to keep your mouth closed, to notice the rise and fall of your belly. Experience what natural breathing feels like. ■

As natural breathing becomes more instinctive for you, you can apply it to sport and life. Your breath becomes timed rhythmically to the force and rhythm of your movements, providing a greater measure of grace and ease. Ultimately, you will begin to feel that your breath moves your body, freeing you from unnecessary muscular effort. Whenever you feel tense, take a relaxed breath. As the children's rhyme goes, *"Breathe in the good stuff, breathe out the bad stuff, set your troubles free."* Feel the pleasure of slow, deep, relaxed breathing. Let the shoulders hang. In a few moments, you'll feel the change. Controlling the breath is one of the ways you can harness the power of emotions.

Expanding Awareness

The law of accommodation reminds us that "in life, development follows demand." In contrast, *what isn't used becomes obsolete.* On the physical level, for example, if you don't use a muscle, it atrophies — it becomes weak. It's the same for reactive emotional habit patterns; through nonuse, they become obsolete.

Witnessing is a learned skill consisting of recognition and release of old patterns. If you notice anger, you acknowledge it and accept it. It may seem strange, but you can feel good physically no matter what negative thoughts or emotions arise. Negative thoughts don't have to mean negative tension — if you remember to breathe, shake loose, and relax. This is the essence of witnessing.

Acknowledging an emotional obstruction — "I'm afraid," "I feel angry" — seems essential for optimal health. But obsessing on fear, habitually dramatizing it, and struggling to fix it only reinforces the obstruction. Instead, pay attention to *doing* whatever you are doing with elegance.

Fear, anger, and sorrow are all parts of life. You can't make them go away by wishing it. Emotions pass like clouds in the sky. Meanwhile, you always have the power to choose how you will respond. You may feel afraid, but you don't have to behave fearfully. Emotions are not destiny.

As a famous boxing coach, said, "Heroes and cowards feel the same fear; heroes just act differently."

CHAPTER SIX

Physical Talent

*Ambition by itself never gets anywhere until it forms a
partnership with hard work.*
— *James Garfield*

To many athletes seeking the mental edge, working with the
mind and emotions seems to promise an easy way to success. But as Thomas Edison said, "Most people miss opportunity because it's dressed in overalls and looks like work."

As mental clarity lights the path and emotional energy fur-
nishes the fuel, your body provides the vehicle for action.

Even if you understand the road and your tank is full, you
need a vehicle to take the journey. Golfers with clear minds and
inspired emotions still have to learn to swing the club if they
are going to play well. *It all comes down to what you actually
do.*

*Success is sweet, but it usually has the scent
of sweat about it.*
— *Anonymous*

Your Most Prized Possession

Take a moment to appreciate your body — or take a lifetime.
There is no greater miracle in nature. Its complexities fill
libraries, and still there's more to be discovered. Just as the universe contains millions of bodies, your body contains millions of

universes — you are made of the same stuff as stars. Each time you breathe, you are breathing in molecules breathed out by Jesus, Mohammed, the Buddha.

Your body's brain can contemplate the cosmos over breakfast, write a sonnet over tea. And if there is a cosmic instruction manual, the first rule is surely that we each receive a body. It is the *only* thing we are guaranteed to keep for a lifetime — not our house, our car, our money, our relationships, our friends, or even our beliefs.

Whatever our beliefs, we can only know *for certain* that we have *this* life, *this* body. Its warranty is limited — good for a short time. So let's look at the body's care, feeding, and development.

Leverage for Change

Because our mind and emotions are difficult to observe and tend to resist change, the body is an ideal, highly visible medium for transformation. And developing and caring for the body also helps the mind and emotions. When you relax the body and release tensions, the mind and emotions reflect this change — and vice versa. Physical training uses the visible to mold the invisible.

Our knowledge of fitness is incomplete. We are even now rediscovering ancient body wisdom from the Eastern traditions, particularly certain martial arts. We are going deeper into the body, from the outer layers of musculature, into the heart and lungs, and still deeper into the recesses of the nervous system.

Physical fitness of the future will center around forms of conscious exercise that include, or even evolve from, forms of hatha yoga, breathwork, meditation, and ever-more-sophisticated forms of bodywork and refined physical disciplines. These may include Feldenkreis and Alexander work, other deep-tissue massage methods, biofeedback, acupuncture and acupressure, and hundreds of other systems that explore healing and bridge the body mind connection.

We have seen aerobics evolve from high-impact routines to nonimpact, flowing movement, often incorporating sophisticated warmups, cooldowns, deep relaxation, martial arts, and meditation. In the next generation, we will see sports become less competitive, and more cooperatively challenging and sophisticated.

Where *no pain, no gain* was once the norm, aware teachers are now showing how to develop within one's comfort zone, without stress, without cycles of fatigue, strain, and recovery.

> *Exercise is only as beneficial as the posture*
> *in which you perform it.*
> — *Matthias Alexander*

Reshaping the Body

Your body is malleable; you can sculpt it over time with daily habits of diet and exercise. The law of accommodation reminds us that the body may change slowly, but it will change. Training for body mind mastery means aligning the body's shape and movements to natural forces. Look, for example, at your body's relationship to gravity. There are only two stable positions in gravity: horizontal and vertical. If your body is lying flat or standing straight, it's naturally aligned in gravity. If the body is out of line — if it has poor posture — then extra energy is required to keep it stable in the pull of gravity. To maintain an off-balance position you need to lean on something, or else exert muscular effort.

Take a moment to stand up; then lean forward, sideward, or backward a few degrees, from the waist — or just stick your head forward a few inches. You'll soon feel a pressure or slight tension in the muscles now working to hold the spine vertical. If you held that position for a few minutes or more, it would become painful.

GETTING STRAIGHT

For ten minutes, while sitting, standing, or moving, see if you can maintain a tall, stretched, erect posture, with a long back, chin gently tucked in, the back of your head stretched upward, and shoulders relaxed. Notice whether this is easy or difficult for you. ■

If you're like most of us, your body is probably out of line, deviating to some degree from perfect vertical alignment. This misalignment can be a result of childhood accidents, incorrect movement patterns and compensations, occupational or sports imbalances, even emotional traumas that created stored tensions and shortened muscles.

Aggressive people often hold their heads or chins slightly forward because of chronic tension and shortened muscles in the back of the neck. If you injured an ankle years ago and began to favor it, you may have caused compensatory reactions up through the knees, hips, and shoulders. Some people follow a pattern of holding the belly in or pulling the pelvis back, each causing misalignment in gravity.

These or similar postural imbalances result in chronic tension. Energy is wasted, since muscular effort is constantly required to hold the body up. Postural imbalance is a major source of energy drain.

Chronic physical tension may go unnoticed, since you become accustomed to it over the years, but it results in a continual sense of discomfort, with shifting and fidgeting, nervousness, and even emotional irritability. When our body feels uncomfortable to live in, we have no other place to go.

Many systems of massage, exercise, and manipulation can aid your conscious efforts to realign your body. If your connective tissue has become shortened as a result of chronic tension, *trying* to have good posture will do little good, because as soon as you relax, the shortened tissue will pull the body parts into the habitually misaligned position. In many cases, therefore, deep tissue work and chiropractic manipulation can make a positive difference. While massage uses pressure and stroking to temporarily relax and release chronic tension, *deep tissue massage* works with lengthening the fascia or connective tissue around the muscles, for more lasting results.

Conscious Exercise

Unlike most outer-directed sports and games centered around points and scores, conscious exercise is inner-directed — specifically designed for overall balance and the well-being of the body, mind, and emotions.

If you're very strong but inflexible, hatha yoga, dance, or other forms of stretching practice will serve to extend your range of motion. On the other hand, if you're naturally flexible, specific strength-building exercises will better serve your overall balance through muscular control and joint stability. Our bodies respond naturally to well-balanced and regular exercise.

HANGING: BALANCING GRAVITY'S CRUNCH

Without gravity, you'd soon become a mass of mush, without muscle tone, with weak circulation of blood and lymph, totally susceptible to any unusual stresses on the body. The field of gravity is the *great developer*, a twenty-four-hour exercise laboratory. Astronauts must exercise or create artificial gravity to avoid weakening bones and muscles.

On the other hand, gravity's pull can also be debilitating. You are being compressed all day; the vertebrae are pressed, one against the other, with only small pads between them, and your feet bear the great burden of your entire body weight. Gravity compresses your joints hour after hour.

The simplest way to balance gravity's crunch is to hang every day. In the morning and evening, grab hold of a bar or solid door sill, or make a simple hanging bar that will easily support your weight. Hang for ten seconds to a half minute. Feel the joints opening, the spine gently stretching out. ■

Resistance to Change

Our bodies, like our minds and emotions, have a tendency to resist change. We settle into certain patterns of movement and behavior — called "psychosclerosis," hardening of the attitudes.

Such resistance is related to Newton's law of inertia and momentum, which states, "A body at rest tends to stay at rest, and a body in motion tends to stay in motion, unless acted upon by external force." Equally true, a body in balance tends to stay in balance, and a body out of balance tends to stay that way, too, unless acted upon by an outside force.

Any change, therefore, requires an initial period of discomfort, until the body adjusts to the new demand. The discomfort may be mild in some cases, like the hunger pangs you feel when you improve your diet, or it may be more severe, as in the withdrawal symptoms of quitting a drug habit. In any case, symptoms are signs of the body readjusting; they will pass.

This initiatory period of change may last from one to six weeks, or even longer. Unless the desire to change remains strong, body and mind tend to return to old, familiar patterns. It takes time — from three to six months — for old habits to become obsolete. By the end of that time, you'll have adapted to a new pattern. In a sense, you'll have found a new way of life.

The laws of process, balance, and natural order all point to the obvious: You absolutely can reshape your life patterns and body through insight, direction, and energy — when mind and emotions work under the dominion of the will.

Feeding the Physical Self

Your body is fed on many levels — through sunlight and fresh air, through peaceful environments, through affection and energy from friends and family, as well as through the food you eat. All these factors are equally important for us to thrive as a complete human being, but the food you eat has a great influence on your body's shape, function, and talent. These are important principles to remember:

- *How* you eat is as important as *what* you eat.
- Emotional calm, proper eating habits, and eating at the appropriate times and places are as important to consider as the food itself. That doesn't mean we have to become nutritional scientists. Even young children will choose by instinct the proper combination of foods for balanced nutrition if offered a variety.
- Precivilized humans ate whatever foods were in season, when they were fresh, without chemical additives, preservatives, or commercial processing. The processing, preserving, coloring, and sweetening that characterize many foods today are practices designed to make higher profits by preventing spoilage and attracting buyers. Whether all this processing ultimately adds or detracts from the quality of the food you eat remains controversial, as one study contradicts

another. (The results seem oddly dependent upon who is sponsoring the study.) Most objective nutritionists concede fresh, unprocessed, locally grown food that is in season best sustains vitality. Study the literature, but above all trust your instincts.

- Many experts know a lot about the nutritional value of various foods, but *you* are the expert on your own body. Nutritious food like whole wheat bread may not be good for you if you happen to be allergic to wheat gluten, for example.

- The reason so many of us need reshaping in the first place is because we tend to eat too much of what we *don't* need and not enough of what we *do* need.

- Notice the difference between what you *want* and what you *need*. Pay attention not just to how the food tastes but to how you feel after you eat it.

- Many athletes find they feel better — lighter, with better endurance — by eating less meat, less animal protein. The belief that an athlete (or anyone) needs lots of protein is a myth. Every protein-related health problem in medical records relates to too much protein, not too little. If you consume sufficient calories and a variety of foods, you will get plenty of protein. The world's top endurance athletes eventually learn that a normal diet with a variety of foods — focusing on whole grains, vegetables, and fruits — gives them a winning edge in sport and life.

John Robbins, author of the classic book *Diet for a New America*, helped dispel the myth that athletes need meat. He describes athletes like Dave Scott, of Davis, California, who won Hawaii's legendary Ironman Triathlon a record four times. Many consider Dave Scott the fittest man who ever lived. Scott is a vegetarian.

Sixto Linares, also a vegetarian, broke the world record for a "double Ironman" — in one day — by swimming 4.8 miles, cycling 185 miles, then running 52.4 miles. Robert Sweetgall of

Newark, Delaware, the world's premier ultra-distance walker, is another vegetarian. So is Edwin Moses, a *Sports Illustrated* Sportsman of the Year.

You might not expect to find a vegetarian in world championship bodybuilding competitions, but Andreas Cahling, 1980 Mr. International, is a vegetarian, and has been for over ten years of competing at the highest international level. Robbins cites a great many other examples of sports champions in many fields who do not eat meat.

In college, while recovering from a serious motorcycle accident, I stopped eating meat. I was the only one of my teammates who even considered such a "radical" course. My coach assured me it was just a fad; my doctor told me I needed meat to help my leg recover. But my dietary change felt so right that I trusted my instincts. A year later, as one of the strongest gymnasts in the nation, I helped lead my team to the National Collegiate Championships. Now, thirty years later, my coach tells me he's eating less meat.

Although you may not choose a completely vegetarian diet, if you simplify your diet in the direction of fresh, natural, unprocessed foods, pay attention to your instincts, your body will become more sensitive, and you won't need me or anyone else to tell you what you should eat. You'll begin to want to eat just what you need, instead of needing to eat everything you want.

It isn't easy to eat well; it isn't always convenient. You therefore have to clearly understand how your dietary patterns affect your life. But knowledge isn't enough, as evidenced by those of us who are in poor health from eating what we *know* we shouldn't have. You can sensitize yourself by paying attention to what you put into your mouth and how you feel afterward. Then act on your understanding.

In addition to diet, we also need to balance our habits of posture, breathing, and rest if we are to achieve optimum vitality. This vitality in turn gives us the power to develop our physical talent.

The Four Ss of Physical Talent

Physical talent is composed of four primary qualities, each of which begins with the letter S: *strength, suppleness, stamina,* and *sensitivity*. When we call someone talented, we are pointing to these four key elements. Most learning blocks encountered in games, music, dance, or martial arts, are related to a deficiency in one or more of these four aspects of physical talent.

As you develop and integrate strength, suppleness, stamina, and sensitivity, you raise your potential — you become more talented. We often call talented athletes *gifted*, as if they were given their prowess as a birthday gift.

Although your genetic makeup does contribute toward your overall potential, preparation and work have a far greater influence on talent than genetics. At birth you have potential; what you do with it is up to you. I've seen many gifted athletes fall by the wayside because of lack of desire, interest, and direction. I've also seen athletes that few people would call gifted go on to develop high levels of talent and success; in other words, they changed themselves from slow learners to fast learners by elevating their levels of strength, suppleness, stamina, and sensitivity.

Let's take a look at each of the four Ss to appreciate your current, and potential, levels of talent. Before you do, however, it's essential to understand the master key that unlocks all four of these fundamental building blocks.

Relaxation: The Master Key to Physical Talent

> *The less effort, the faster and more powerful you will be.*
> — *Bruce Lee*

There's a story about a man who continually sought more energy and light in his life. Finally he climbed a sacred mountain and cried up to the heavens, "Fill me full of light!"

A voice thundered down through the clouds, "I'm always filling you, but you keep leaking!"

One of the worst things about tension is that it leaks energy.

Relaxation, in contrast, enhances strength, suppleness, stamina, and sensitivity. By the end of this chapter, you'll understand how and why.

Studies of efficiency in movement carried out at several universities showed that people tend to waste effort and create unnecessary muscular tension in even the simplest movements, such as lifting a fork, holding a book, sitting in a chair. Not only did the subjects use more tension than necessary, they also tensed muscles that were unrelated to the movements being made.

Now, as your body gets used to relaxing — in stillness and motion — you more easily notice tension as it begins to develop, and you have the power to release it. This represents a giant step on the path to body mind mastery.

Relaxation is the best single indicator of your well-being. Your degree of relaxation across the three centers — physical, mental, and emotional — precisely reflects your alignment with the natural laws. Physical ease is a mirror of the relationship of body to mind. When you are truly relaxed and centered, the mind comes to rest, the emotions flow clearly, and the vital body surrenders itself to nature's flow. All feels right with the world, because all feels right with the body.

> *Your ability to relax reflects your willingness to trust.*
> *— Anonymous*

Most of us have carried subtle tensions for so many years that we've forgotten what real relaxation is. Rather than a temporary state achieved by dissipating knotted energy, it is a continual enjoyment of muscular release and high energy at the same time.

It does little good for me to advise people to relax until they know what relaxation feels like and they become aware of the degree of tension they carry.

TESTING FOR RELAXATION

Ask a friend to lift your arm as you endeavor to let it hang limp. Notice whether or not you unconsciously help your friend lift your arm, or whether your arm is totally dead weight. Do this experiment with a friend, and you'll notice how some people, as a result of chronic, unconscious, and energy-wasting tension they carry with them all day, cannot let their arms relax, try as they might. ■

A relaxed arm should shake like jelly when someone takes your hand in both his or her hands and shakes vigorously. If your arm is lifted and released, it should drop to your side instantly. If you carry a lot of tension (as many older people do, having stored it over the years), the arm may even stay in place for a long moment before dropping.

If the preceding exercise helped you become aware of the chronic tension you carry, the following exercise will provide the means to release it, over time, by creating an experience of profound relaxation.

*"When you cannot see
what is happening,
do not stare harder.
Relax and look gently
with your inner eye."*
— *Lao Tzu*

DEEP RELAXATION EXERCISE

Lie on your back on a carpet or mattress, and loosen any tight clothing. Have a friend read the following instructions to you, or else record them yourself and play them back. Once you know the steps and your body gets accustomed to this state, you can easily go through the process anytime, even in a few minutes.

Be aware of the body's weight. Breathing slowly and naturally, surrender to gravity. Notice the floor pressing up against the body and the body pressing equally down into the floor.

Put your attention on your feet . . . imagine they are very heavy. Feel the skin heavy, the bones heavy . . . the whole body becoming heavy.

Feel the deep, profound heaviness spreading up into your lower legs and through the knees, releasing all the muscles. Feel the lower legs heavy . . . the skin heavy, the bones heavy . . . the whole body becoming heavy.

Feel the heaviness continue into the thighs and buttocks. Feel all the muscles of the thighs release and the buttocks relax, feel the skin heavy, the bones heavy . . . the whole body becoming heavy.

Let the pleasant heaviness sink deep into the lower back, releasing . . . and continue into the upper back, around and under the shoulder blades, along the spine . . . releasing . . . heavy. Let the muscles of the upper back and neck and shoulders sink into gravity's pull . . . skin heavy, bones heavy . . . the whole body heavy.

Let go of the upper arms . . . the elbows and lower arms . . . feel the heaviness all the way to the fingertips . . . skin, bones . . . the whole body . . . heavy.

Feel all the muscles of the neck . . . front, back, and sides . . . release and sink to the floor . . . skin, bones . . . the whole body heavy.

Now the entire body below the neck is heavy, totally relaxed. If you feel any tension left anywhere, let it go, and become twice as heavy.

Now, as I name the areas of the face and scalp, feel them as heavy, and let them go with gravity . . . skin, bones . . . the whole body . . . heavy.

Feel the scalp release . . . all the muscles of the forehead . . . around the eye sockets . . . the cheeks, letting go . . . the muscles around the nose . . . the mouth and jaw, all releasing . . . the chin, and around the ears.

Now your entire body is in deep relaxation. Energies flow through the body freely, revitalizing, healing, rebalancing.

Notice your breathing. Imagine you're floating gently, on your own warm, private ocean. On inhalation, feel yourself float slowly up, and on exhalation, float back down . . . feeling the well-being of total relaxation.

Imagine the blood coursing freely through the body, nourishing it. Feel the energy of the body, vibrating within the cells.

Feel the peacefulness of relaxation. Notice how calm the mind is in this moment — and how open your feelings are. The next time you experience any emotional upset, let the body relax into this pleasant state.

Imagine yourself walking, with this same feeling of release . . . using only the muscular effort you need, and no more. Feel the lightness and effortlessness of running . . . or playing your favorite sport with the same relaxed grace.

As you feel this state, know that you can return to it at will. Now begin to increase the depth of your breathing. Ending with three gigantic breaths of energy, open your eyes, and sit up. Stretch like a cat. ■

Consummate athletes and artists in every field have attained an ease of movement through efficient use of muscles. Dynamic relaxation is the foundation of all physical talent. Now let's examine the four building blocks of talent, beginning with strength.

Strength

> *Nothing is so strong as real gentleness;*
> *nothing is so gentle as real strength.*
> *— Anonymous*

If you had no voluntary muscle tissue, you would spend your brief life as a puddle of protoplasm — a heap of skin, organs, and bones. People with muscular disabilities appreciate that which we take for granted: the ability to move at will.

Any physiologist will tell you that if you stimulate enough muscle fiber for a given demand over a period of time, the body will build larger fiber to meet the demand. Muscular strength increases in proportion to the effort of training. That all seems straightforward. Yet there's more to muscle than meets the eye.

We all appreciate that strength is one of the primary qualities that comprise physical talent. But many of us do not *use* strength most effectively. Strength involves more than the ability to contract muscle tissue; it also involves your ability to control movement.

Many athletes who train intensively for strength develop large, powerful muscles, but may nevertheless have diminished *effective* strength because they are generally tense and haven't "educated" their appropriate muscle groups in complementary tension-relaxation. They therefore can't hit or throw as hard, run as fast, leap as high, or react as quickly as they might.

Since effective strength is the ability to relax the proper muscle groups while consciously tensing others, it should come as no surprise that babies have this ability. Put your finger in a baby's grasp, and try to pull away. Those little hands are surprisingly relaxed — and surprisingly powerful.

> *Greatness lies not in being strong*
> *but in the right use of strength.*
> — *Anonymous*

One study compared the movement abilities of six-month-old babies and some professional football players. The athletes tried to copy every movement and posture of these babies for ten full minutes without stopping. Not a single athlete could keep up; they all dropped out from exhaustion within a few minutes.

Bodybuilders may appear to be the strongest athletes in terms of weight they can lift, but in the economies of strength, women gymnasts, who have less muscle bulk, embody effective strength in action. And look at the cat! You don't see any muscle-bound cats walking around, yet what athlete can match a cat's movement? I've seen cats jump ten feet straight up from a sitting position. A cat can be soundly napping, then instantly spring after a mouse with blinding speed, then, just as suddenly, stop and clean its paws, totally relaxed. The cat carries very little tension. You can squeeze its muscle to the bone, and it will show no pain. Try squeezing *your* calf muscles to the bone, and feel the tension.

Various exercise systems emphasize relaxation-in-movement as a primary objective. One such system, called eurythmics, involves the gradual tensing and relaxing of different parts of the body to a regular rhythm, coordinated with the breath, while maintaining complete relaxation of the rest of the body. It's possible to eventually master the conscious tensing of twelve different parts of the body independently.

To experience relaxed strength, try the following exercise from the martial art of Aikido. This exercise is done with a partner, who will gradually attempt to bend your arm twice — the first time against your resistance, the second time against your nonresistance. Whether your partner can bend your arm in both or neither of the attempts is unimportant. Instead, feel the difference between "relaxed strength" and "tense strength."

UNBENDABLE ARM

Test 1. Hold your right arm out in front of you, first clenched, arm slightly bent, with your wrist on your partner's shoulder. Your partner puts one hand on the crook of your elbow and gradually begins to push down, in order to bend your arm (in the direction it normally bends, of course). You resist, tensing your arm.

Shake your arm loose before Test 2.

Test 2. Standing balanced, place your wrist on your partner's shoulder as before, this time with your fingers extended and spread.

Your partner will again begin pushing downward gradually, as if to bend your arm.

This time, however, you'll remain free of tension. Let your arm be totally relaxed, yet strong — not like a wet noodle. You do this by imagining a powerful flow of energy, like water gushing through a hose, continually flowing through your arm and out the ends of your extended fingers, shooting right through the wall for a thousand miles.

Let your awareness flow with the energy, continuing past your partner's arm. As your partner begins to push more, imagine an increase in the power of the flow balancing the pressure.

Experiment with this exercise, and see if you begin to feel a new kind of relaxed strength. ■

With a little practice, your arm becomes nearly unbendable when relaxed and actually weaker when tensed. It works because you are using your muscles more efficiently — tensing only those muscle-groups you need. This develops effective strength with greater ease.

This next exercise highlights the way your mind can influence effective strength.

TENSION PUSH-UPS

You will do two push-ups with more tension, and two with less tension.

1. Beginning from an up position, do two push-ups at a slow-to-moderate pace, with every muscle in your body tensed. This is what it's like to *try*. Clench your teeth, tighten your thighs, buttocks, stomach, neck. It's exhausting, and makes the push-ups seem difficult, right?

To a lesser extent, this is what most athletes do during training, because they haven't practiced conscious relaxation-in-movement.

2. For the second two push-ups, imagine that you're a puppet on a string, suspended from the arms of a giant standing directly over you. The giant will do the work for you. Starting from the same up position, just relax down effortlessly, and imagine the giant pulling you up on the strings. Let the push-up happen by itself. ■

By using the image of "energy flow" or "movement happening by itself" in these two exercises, you create the psychophysical effect of relaxed strength, and all three centers — physical, mental, and emotional — fall into a natural relationship.

Strength, then, works best in a state of dynamic relaxation. The height you can jump from a standing position is a result of both your ability to relax and your ability to then push and spring. Try standing up, crouching down, tensing your legs as hard as you can, and jumping — you can hardly move.

Dale was captain of the Stanford gymnastics team. He was a floor-exercise and tumbling specialist, and was one of the hardest workers on the team. Each day, Dale would begin with calisthenics, then squat jumps for leg strength; he ran about three miles every day; he practiced his tumbling sequences over and over and over. His legs were well-muscled and his diet excellent. He was slim, yet in his tumbling he looked like he weighed five hundred pounds; he just couldn't seem to get up into the air. A few beginning tumblers with legs like toothpicks would run out and tumble higher than he could. It used to drive him crazy.

Dale had plenty of muscle but too much tension. Besides, muscle weighs more than fat; those who must move quickly and lightly need light, sinewy muscles rather than large, bulky ones. Training with lighter weights but more repetitions works best for gymnasts, martial artists, and dancers, for example.

Your muscles develop in response to demand. Balance the demand for sheer power with relaxation. The next summer, Dale spent time performing relaxation and quickness drills, and his tumbling showed dramatic improvement.

By practicing dynamic relaxation, your movements, too, will show more grace with less effort, leading to improved speed, coordination, balance, rhythm, timing, and reflex speed in sport and life.

Suppleness

Suppleness is the embodiment of nonresistance.

For most of us, developing suppleness requires stretching exercises. Yet a baby needs no special exercises because it carries no chronic tension; neither did you, long ago. As you grew, however, you began to unconsciously tense or hold muscles — in your neck, shoulders, back, thighs, and abdomen — in response to physical pain, psychological threat, or emotional upset.

Although thoughts and emotions come and go, they impose tensions on the body — tension that can become habitual or chronic over time. As the years pass, these holding patterns result in stiffness, aches and pains, and limited range of motion. That's when stretching exercises become necessary.

The first step in releasing chronic tension is to become aware that it exists. Notice when you begin to tense; then shake loose and relax. Do this more and more, until relaxation and release become a new habit replacing the old.

Many athletes push and pull their bodies through various extended positions either casually or aggressively, gritting their teeth in pain. This kind of program is a "two steps forward, one step back" approach. It's painful, and it sets up reactive tension (like those who struggle to diet, only to end up bingeing).

The best recipe I know for suppleness combines two parts relaxation with one part stretching. Without doing any stretching, you become more supple when you're relaxed, on vacation, or free from your usual concerns.

If you ask your body to grow more supple, it will, but you must ask nicely. The following guidelines are polite ways to ask your body to stretch. Your body is like a young child — make courteous, gentle requests, and you'll receive greater cooperation.

WHOLE BODY STRETCH

1. When it comes to your own body, you are the stretching expert. You know more about precisely where, and to what degree, you need to stretch than anyone else, for the body in question is yours.

Whenever you feel tight, move into a slightly more extended range of motion than you're used to. That sounds almost too simple, but that's what stretching entails. You don't need to be an expert on anatomy — just feel where it's tight and stretch there. Breathe deeply, and imagine the breath going directly to the tightness, and releasing it. Be gentle and patient.

2. Generally it's best to stay relaxed when stretching, but you'll make even more progress if you deliberately tense and work the muscles *against* the direction of the stretch as you stretch, and then follow it by relaxing once again.

3. There are two kinds of stretching: stretching like a cat waking from a nap and intense stretching to increase range of motion. Cat stretching should be pleasurable, while intense stretching will naturally involve

some discomfort. The key is to balance between pleasure and pain.

4. Only stretch a little, but do it every day. It's better
to do three or four minutes of relaxed stretching every
day than fifteen minutes of grinding it out, once or twice
a week. Ask the body nicely, but ask it often.

5. Stretch when the body is warm. It's easier, it feels
better, and it does more good. Cold stretching hurts
more — and you're more likely to be tense.

6. Experiment and trust your instincts as to what
style of stretch works best for you, and how long to
hold a stretch. ■

Besides "The Peaceful Warrior Warm-up" you'll soon learn,
I offer no specific stretching exercises here; you can determine
what your body needs for your own activities. What movements do you normally perform in training and daily life?
Work on that range of motion.

The object of stretching is to open and free all joints,
depending on the needs of your favorite activities. As you
become supple beyond the actual point of need, you also
extend your range of power, since the more supple you are, the
less energy you need to expend in order to move.

If you would like to pursue greater flexibility in your body
and your life you might enroll in a class in yoga, T'ai Chi, gymnastics, or dance. One of the best books on the subject is
Stretching, by Bob Anderson.

Freedom from Lower Back Pain

Lower back pain, a complaint so common as to be nearly universal, may originate in mental, emotional, or situational stress

related to business, relationships, or other concerns, but the
five most common physical sources of lower back pain include:

1. Weak abdominal muscles
2. Stiff lower back
3. Weak lower back
4. Tight hamstrings (back of knees)
5. Tight quadriceps (front of thighs)

By strengthening and stretching these areas, you can reduce
or eliminate most lower back pain. Chiropractic and deep-
tissue massage can help relieve some of the tension and imbalances that cause pain but will not usually last without applied
stretching and strength work in these key areas, which allow
for proper postural alignment in the field of gravity.

Suppleness, strength, and relaxation are intimately related.
To become natural, movement requires all three. No amount of
strength will freely move a stiff joint. If you want to lift your
leg high into the air to do a dance step, kick a football, or perform a gymnastics movement, you need both the strength to lift
the leg and the suppleness to allow the full range of muscle
motion. Effective movement always requires the integration
and balance of suppleness and strength.

Suppleness developed through awareness of tension, conscious relaxation, and proper stretching will improve your
game and decrease muscle pulls, sprains, and related injuries. It
will increase the muscle's responsiveness through increased circulation. You'll feel more youthful, awake, and alive in daily
life as your range of movement increases. You can become
more supple at forty, fifty, or sixty than you were in high
school.

As you remember to relax into life, moment to moment,
you'll become more supple. As you increase your suppleness,
you'll relax more easily. You'll also notice another change: an
increase in sensitivity, which we examine now.

Sensitivity

A master of T'ai Chi was so sensitive to the forces around him that if a fly landed on his shoulder, he would sway gently under its impact. Legend has it that a sparrow was unable to jump from his open palm and fly, because as it pushed away, his hand would sink beneath its legs. Such sensitivity reflects our own potential, refined through practice.

Sensitivity includes all our five senses of sight, hearing, taste, smell, and touch. But balance and kinesthetic awareness are most relevant to athletes. Sensitivity to our inner and outer environments allows for greater coordination between mind and muscle, and between our various body parts.

Someone with excellent coordination also has superior timing and rhythm, along with refined balance and fast reflexes. Coordination, balance, timing, rhythm, and reflex speed are all interrelated forms of sensitivity, which allow faster learning and greater capacity.

If you concentrate on one aspect of sensitivity, such as balance, the other aspects will also develop. This is one reason it's wise to expose yourself to a variety of movement activities. Wise golfers, tennis players, or other athletes take beginning gymnastics, dance, hatha yoga, or martial arts. All demand more refined balance, suppleness, and relaxation and will improve their chances of success both in sport and the dynamic challenges of everyday life.

Beyond what I've already outlined, you don't have to do anything to achieve greater sensitivity, for it improves naturally as you remember to relax and *pay attention*.

Sensitivity enables more efficient learning because your body picks up cues faster — you feel errors and correct them more quickly. Your skill at imitating the experts improves, because you open the circuits between mind and movement. You free yourself from old patterns of tension as you become sensitive to them. But you have to recognize an error before you can correct it. Try this experiment to discover how relaxation enhances sensitivity:

RELAXATION AND SENSITIVITY

Test 1. Look around you and find two nearby objects of different weight, such as a paperweight and a pencil.

First tense your arm and hands — right out to your fingertips — as tense and tight as you can. In this state of tension, pick up one object and put it down, then pick up the other object and put it down. You'll note that it is almost impossible to sense the different weights.

Test 2. Next, shake your arm loose and let it relax as much as possible. Then pick the objects up, one after the other. This time, notice how easy it is to sense the difference in weight. ∎

Under normal conditions, you'll probably never be as tense as in the first part of this test. But on more subtle levels, even a small amount of tension interferes with refined balance, timing, coordination, and reflex speed. The body mind master, like the cat, is a paragon of apparent contrasts — capable of unleashing awesome power, yet so soft, smooth, and sensitive that he or she can recognize the most subtle cues.

It takes more than running out and playing blindly to develop a foundation of natural physical talent. First, reestablish a natural order of training, beginning with relaxation, the master key to talent. Then develop strength without wasting energy. Free of unnecessary tension, you can then develop flowing suppleness. Combined strength and suppleness then form a foundation of sensitivity and you achieve excellence with greater ease.

Still, learning skills requires practice, and practice requires stamina. We now turn to stamina, the fourth key to physical talent.

Stamina

No athlete ever became an expert without investing time and energy. So stamina — or the ability to work over a period of time — is a cornerstone of talent.

Stamina mirrors the law of accommodation: that demand over time develops desired qualities. It takes stamina to perform any action over an extended period of time. Writing a book, for example, requires a kind of stamina different from running a marathon. Anyone caught in rush-hour traffic or long lines at the bank needs mental and emotional forms of stamina.

Stamina is a natural response to training. If you place a demand on your lungs and heart to bring oxygen to the tissues more rapidly, they'll accommodate. If you make a demand on your muscles to work for longer periods of time, they'll adapt to that demand.

Stamina is interrelated with relaxation, strength, and suppleness. As you release chronic tension and relax, you improve stamina. With greater effective strength, you can work more over a longer time. As you become supple, you move through greater range with less energy. It takes time to get into shape, but not as much time as some of us fear.

Lawrence Morehouse, a UCLA researcher, with other colleagues has found that in six weeks of inactivity, you can lose eighty percent of your conditioning. *And* in six more weeks of progressive training, you can also regain 80 percent of your peak condition.

You don't have to hurt to develop stamina. The jogger who trains for two weeks, running one and a half miles on level ground, and then decides to start running hills for three miles is forgetting natural order. Apply patience; develop stamina gradually. You'll inevitably get to your desired level of fitness, based on how long you continue progressive training, not how quickly you do so. Getting in shape can be an invigorating, pleasurable activity or a masochistic experience, depending on your degree of patience. You shouldn't try to rush into shape any more than a seed would rush to grow into a tree. Some adjustments, and even discomfort, are a natural part of the process as your body accommodates to greater capacity, but if it feels like agony, then you need to slow down and stop "pushing the river."

How to Avoid Athletic Injuries

Injuries are the plague of athletes. The pain involved is the least of it. A single injury, whether chronic or acute, can undo months or years of training, or may even end a career prematurely. Injuries often leave a trace of tension and fear in the body, and it negates the primary purpose of sport — health and well-being.

Injury most often results from a fundamental flaw in our talent foundation (of strength, suppleness, stamina, and sensitivity), or from impatience, a lack of attention, or some combination of these. "Accidents" aren't really accidents.

To avoid injuries, you need mental clarity and attention, emotional stability, and physical preparation. They are the three best insurance policies you'll ever have — and they don't cost a cent.

Acute injury resulting from an impact (a fall, collision, or blow) or from a movement beyond the body's limits of tolerance (a torque or twist) occur more rarely than chronic injuries — those developed over periods of time through improper training or insufficient preparation. Body mind training helps eliminate both kinds of injury by preventing their causes.

In order to highlight for you some of the major causes of injury — mental, emotional, and physical — I'm going to create a character named Jerry who exhibits all the pitfalls that create injuries. Jerry sprained his ankle and can't understand how this happened.

Mental factors. Jerry is easily distracted, either by his own thoughts or by activities around him. He thinks of himself as "klutzy." He has a habit of criticizing himself mercilessly and tends to punish himself through pain. He has conflicts about competing and the season is about to begin.

Emotional factors. Jerry relies on motivation to apply himself, but his motivation rises and falls. Sometimes he's enthusiastic; other times he'd just as soon sit on the sidelines. He hates getting hit, so he tenses up at the wrong times. Sometimes he hangs back and hesitates. Sometimes he gets angry and stomps around paying no attention to the game around him.

Physical factors. Jerry's ankles are stiff and relatively weak. Because of general tension, he's insensitive to fatigue and on some days pushes himself too far; he's overweight and in poor general condition.

Jerry should be glad he only sprained his ankle.

Looking back on the few athletic injuries I've inflicted on myself, I see the reasons clearly now and have been able to avoid further trauma since. Most were caused by "knowing but not doing" — like when you know you shouldn't lift a heavy object, but you do it anyway. You knew you shouldn't have played when you were tired or distracted, but you decided, "What the heck."

Injury is the price paid for insensitivity, impatience, or inattention.

Body Mind Balance

I've now surveyed the meaning of talent and the way it can be developed in the arenas of mind, emotions, and movement. When I first came upon this holistic approach to athletic training, I was surprised to learn that paying attention to something like breathing could open the way to better balance or greater effective strength, because of the breath's influence on body and mind and emotions. Yet it works. The following exercise shows how the mind can help the body to be centered and grounded.

CONNECTION TO THE EARTH

Tense: Stand stiffly, breathing in the upper chest, with shoulders raised. Feel the tension. If a problem is bothering you, think about it.

Have a partner stand in front of you and reach under your armpits with his or her hands and lift you an inch or two off the floor as you rest your hands on his or her biceps. Remain stiff and tense with shallow breathing as he or she lifts you.

(It doesn't matter whether or not your partner is actually able to lift you, as long as you both feel the difference between the first and second attempts.)

Centered: Next, shake loose and relax. Put your awareness in your lower belly and legs. Feel physically heavy and stable, like a lazy cat or a sleeping baby. Let your shoulders hang down. Imagine your entire lower body is hollow — and then filled with water.

Resting your arms on your partner's arms, ask him or her to lift you in the same way as before — slowly, without any sudden movements. The more he or she lifts, the heavier you become. If you remain relaxed and centered, lifting you will become very difficult, perhaps impossible. You will feel rooted to the ground. ■

This "rooting to the ground" is what the ancient masters of T'ai Chi perfected by developing body mind talent. No one could push them over, yet they could effortlessly toss opponents into the air.

In closing this section, we will examine the unified state.

Satori and Body Mind Mastery

Satori is a word from the Japanese Zen tradition that points to
a "sudden awakening" or insight into our fundamental nature.
This insight is not the result of abstract mental concepts or
ideas but rather a momentary, experiential fusing of body,
mind, and emotions. You experience satori:

- when the mind is free of internal distractions, with attention focused on the present moment;
- when emotional energies flow freely — spontaneous, uninhibited, and expressive — manifesting as motivation; and
- when the body feels vital, relaxed, energized, and sensitive.

The athlete, artist, and musician all experience this state in
the moment of truth. You can, in fact, experience it right now,
with the following exercise.

INSTANT SATORI

Take your keys, a piece of fruit, or any handy object, and
go outside. Throw the object up into the air. Staying
relaxed and easy, catch it. Be sure to catch it. Then come
back inside, and continue reading this exercise.

Now consider the moment the object was in the air.
At that moment you weren't thinking of what you'd have
for dinner or what you did yesterday. You weren't thinking of anything else, either. You may have been attending
to thoughts before you threw it or after you caught it,
but during the throw, you were pure attention, reaching
out, waiting for the object's descent. In that same
moment your emotions were open, and your body was
alert and vitalized — a moment of satori. ∎

This state of body mind integration, inner-outer harmony, feels good on every level; it's the state that athletes describe in glowing metaphors; it's the essence of dynamic meditation and the instinctive reason you enjoy sports; it's the inner target of Zen archers. Satori is the heart of the moving experience, a taste of inner peace and inner power. Over time, it becomes the moment-to-moment practice of body mind mastery.

PART THREE

Body Mind Mastery in Action

Great works are performed
not by speed or strength
but perseverance.
— Samuel Johnson

The most efficient and effective training techniques are aligned with natural law. The combination you see in both martial artists and ballet dancers of strong, stable, lower-body foundations and relaxed, sensitive upper bodies reflects nature's wisdom. Only the tree with strong roots and trunk but flexible, yielding branches will stand up in a hurricane.

As you align your training with the natural laws of accommodation, balance, natural order — and the laws I describe in my book *The Laws of Spirit* — you will begin to master essential technique.

CHAPTER SEVEN

Tools for Training

*What counts is not only the number of hours you put in
but how much you put in those hours.*
— *Anonymous*

Chapter 7 shows how to master technique through natural laws — key principles to enhance and accelerate your learning, principles you can apply to learning any activity.

Warmup and the Transitions of Life

Our lives are filled with cycles and periods of transition. Our growth from infancy through childhood, adolescence, and adulthood required many transitions into increasingly advanced modes of behavior, responsibility, and understanding. Birth and death are the great transitions. Graduation from school, beginning a livelihood, getting married, raising children, and retiring are all lesser but important examples of changes in our lives. Life itself is a series of changes, sometimes smooth and orderly, sometimes unexpected — minute to minute, day to day, year to year. Master athletes need to recognize and accept these periods of transition in training and in life.

Years ago, I used to snap at my wife when I arrived home from work, until I realized that all I needed was a fifteen-minute transition to decompress, slow down, and relax before I was ready to listen happily to her news of the day.

Transitions are in-between periods. When you leave work and are driving home, you're in-between. When golfers hit the ball and are walking down the fairway, they are in-between.

Many of us have difficulties with the transitions of getting up in the morning or going to bed at night. Our minds, emotions, and physical rhythms remain adjusted to an earlier frequency as we begin a new activity requiring much slower or faster vibrations. No wonder we sometimes have difficulty coping with new situations. Instead of leaping out of bed in the morning, you may find it useful to set your alarm fifteen minutes earlier, giving yourself time to glide into the kitchen, put on some water for tea, read a few minutes, look out the window, and take some deep breaths — say hello to a new day. I start my day by sitting up with my eyes still closed, doing a few slow, deep breathing exercises, and drinking a glass of water before I get out of bed.

Learning to make use of these in-between periods will bring more harmony to your life. You can create conscious transitions instead of abrupt changes, shocks, stops, and starts. When you're moving from one activity to another, it may require a different mental, emotional, or physical approach.

Include some light calisthenics, a walk around the block or the Peaceful Warrior Warm-up, as part of your morning transition. The main goal should be to create transition rituals that work for you.

Nowhere are transition rituals so crucial as in athletics. A warm-up serves as a buffer zone between the day's prior events and the moment of athletic truth. A proper warm-up serves to prepare us for the unique demands of sport and helps us prevent days when nothing seems to go right.

Most athletes are familiar with a physical warm-up to warm the muscles, stretch out, and prepare physically for the intensity of training. Relatively few athletes appreciate the importance of a mental and emotional warm-up.

Engaging in mental warm-up means determining a clear course of action for the day. You'll want to choose realistic goals, based on your energy level and the circumstances of the day. Mental warm-up involves turning your attention to the place of practice, leaving all the day's concerns at the door. Finally, you'll want to cultivate the proper attitude of respect and gratitude — the right mindset — for your activity. This is the purpose behind the Zen tradition of bowing upon entering and leaving the practice hall.

Just as a decathlete requires a transition between the pole vault and javelin throw, a gymnast needs a mental transition between two pieces of apparatus requiring different approaches. Even a ballroom dancer needs a transition between a waltz and a foxtrot. Runners and swimmers cultivate different approaches to sprinting and distance events; golfers need different mental warm-ups for driving and putting. Mental warm-up provides the proper focus and energy for each activity.

Emotional warm-up might begin with a few deep, calming breaths. You might recall the initial excitement you first felt about your sport and create mental images to heighten your emotional energy. Focus on what excites you about training. Picture yourself succeeding at your goals.

Mental and emotional warm-up might seem long and involved, but they can actually take place at the speed of thought. The whole process might occur in the space of a few slow, deep breaths or in a moment of quiet contemplation. Many athletes do something like this subconsciously. Mastering body and mind means doing it consciously and strategically to control and amplify your direction and energy for the day.

Physical warm-up doesn't have to be a long, involved process. It is a time to get the body literally warm, oxygenated, fully awake, free of sluggishness — energized and relaxed. Never rush into warm-up; it's not the main event. Your body is like an automobile. You wouldn't want to start a cold engine, then race off at top speed. The oil (or blood) isn't warm and flowing yet.

You may start some days feeling clogged or lethargic. Don't let that discourage you. Some of my all-time best workouts

began like that. It just takes the body longer to warm up on
that kind of day.

After a training session, do some stretching and deep
breathing exercises as a cool-down.

THE PEACEFUL WARRIOR FOUR-MINUTE WARM-UP
FOR SPORT AND LIFE

During my four years at the University of California, I knew
what I would be doing every afternoon. My teammates and I
would begin by running up and down every stairwell and hall-
way in the old Harmon Gymnasium. Then, panting and wheez-
ing, we would enter the gymnastics room and move through a
fast-paced set of strength exercises, including walking on our
hands, and a stretching routine that would make most people
cringe. And this was only the warm-up.

Like many athletes who retire from competition, I stopped
exercising altogether for a while because I failed to appreciate
that my old warm-up alone — never mind the three hours of
training that followed — was sufficient to maintain my vitality
and fitness. So, within a few months of relative inactivity, I
experienced my post-collegiate out-of-shape slump and soon
realized the importance of a consistent warm-up routine.

In the next few pages I present a different kind of warm-up
for sport and life, based upon *The Peaceful Warrior Workout*®
taught in my book, *Everyday Enlightenment*. This warmup,
which takes *less than four minutes*, is a simple and efficient
series of ten flowing movements, featuring deep breathing and
tension release that blend elements of strength, suppleness, stamina, balance, and coordination into an enjoyable, easy-to-do
routine.

Combining elements and energy from yoga, martial arts,
dance, and modern calisthenics, this four-minute series integrates body, breath, and attention to provide an ideal warm-up
for sport and life. It's a great way to help prevent injuries,

enhance physical and mental performance, and prepare you for skiing, bicycling, playing golf or tennis, hiking, or running.

Based on the principle that *a little of something is much better than a lot of nothing*, I recommend this routine to anyone who understands the importance of regular exercise but who hasn't yet begun.

All exercise — whether calisthenics, yoga, dance, gymnastics, or martial arts — combines the elements of *body*, *breath*, and *attention*. The Peaceful Warrior Warm-up develops all three elements. After spending four minutes flowing through this series, you will feel more alert, energized, supple, centered, focused, and expansive. In four minutes you can enhance sports performance or simply jumpstart your day. If you perform this warm-up first thing each day, you will continue to experience the benefits, including a reduction of stress-produced tension, for hours afterward.

General Guidelines

- Exercise is only as good as the posture in which you do it. Pay attention to proper posture and form; check your movements in front of a mirror.
- Each day, strive to refine and improve each movement.
- Make sure you have a clear six-by-six-foot space in which to move.
- Move in a slow, relaxed, conscious manner.
- Pay special attention to breathing deeply, without strain; coordinate your breathing with each movement as indicated. Inhale audibly through the nose; exhale through the nose, mouth, or both.
- Place your feet generally about a shoulder-width apart — sometimes slightly narrower and sometimes wider, depending on what feels best to you.
- To complete the series in less than four minutes, perform each movement one to three times (or more for some of the quicker elements).

BIG STRETCH

Directions

- Inhale up and back; exhale down and forward.
- Keep your palms together in front of you as you raise your arms overhead, then bend and drop them behind your head — stretch gently backwards.
- Straighten your arms and body, then swing your arms forward and down in a wide arc, bending your knees and letting your head drop and relax forward.

- At bottom, your arms then swing back behind you as you momentarily straighten your knees for a stretch, then bend as you —
- Complete the movement by swinging your arms forward and upward as you stand, palms together (into another repetition if desired).
- Remember to bend knees during downswing and up-swing; only straighten legs momentarily at bottom of downswing.

Benefits

- Invigorates entire body while gently stretching the spine.
- Prepares body for exercises to follow.

- Begins to clear tensions around chest and abdomen.

start

finish

SIDE REACH

Directions

- *Inhale* during side reach, *exhale* as you squat.
- With your back straight, squat halfway down with your arms in a "biceps curl" position and tense all your muscles as shown.
- Stretch up directly to one side.

- Squat down as shown, elbows on thighs, then stretch on opposite side.
- Keep weight evenly balanced.
- Let your hips move in the opposite direction of arms.
- Face front squarely with upper elbow behind ear.

Benefits

- Opens ribcage and expands lungs.
- Sideward stretch of the spine.

- Generates vitality.
- Clears energy around the head and shoulder areas.

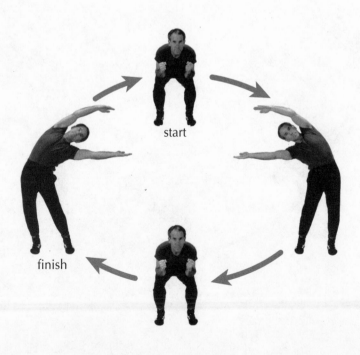

start

finish

NECK RELEASE

Directions

- *Inhale* continuously as head makes three full circles to the left ending in position as shown; then *exhale* fully as head relaxes down to front in preparation to again *inhale* for three circles in the opposite direction.
- Keep head relaxed as it circles; let weight of head provide the stretch and next release.

- Keep teeth closed but not clenched.
- Keep shoulders still and even as head makes relaxed circles.
- At the end of the long, three-circle inhale, as the head rolls to the side and slightly back as shown, the lungs should be completely full of air.

Benefits

- Relaxes tensions of jaw, neck, and shoulders.
- Opens the lungs.

- Clears tensions related to the weight of responsibility.

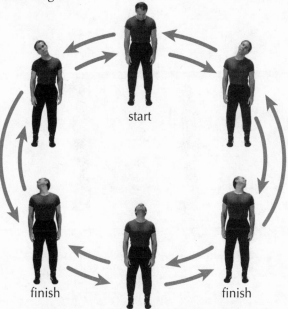

start

finish

finish

Three head circles finishing in position shown

SHOULDER ROLL

Directions

- *Inhale* forward-upward, *exhale* backward-downward.
- Circle shoulders forward-upward-backward-downward.
- Grasp one wrist with other hand.

- Keep arms relaxed and passive; let shoulders move.

Benefits

- Releases tension around the chest, shoulders, and upper back.
- Invigorates and frees movement of upper thorax.

- Clears emotional tension around the heart.

start   finish

SPINE SWING

Directions

- *Inhale* while pulling arm back, *exhale* rapidly while turning back toward center.
- Hold your arms straight and sideward at shoulder height, forming a straight line as if a broomstick were tied to both arms.
- Turn upper body only; keep hips squarely to the front.

- Exhale rapidly so you have time to inhale around to the other side.
- Keep knees relaxed and slightly flexed.
- Head turns to look behind you at your hand as arm pulls back.

Benefits

- Benefits internal pelvic organs.
- Prevents atrophy of lower spine (associated with aging).

- Clears energy field from knees to top of head.
- Increases vitality.

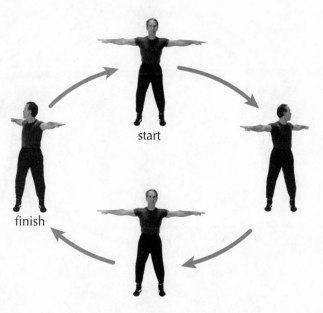

HIP CIRCLES

Directions

- *Inhale* continuously as pelvis circles three times in one direction; *exhale* continuously as pelvis circles three times in opposite direction.

- Keep knees relaxed with head tall and still.
- Let hands rest on hips as shown.
- Pelvis moves in circular movement.

Benefits

- Frees movement of the pelvis.
- Releases tension in lower back and hip connectors.

- Aids digestion by moving intestines.
- Opens energy field from knees to navel.

HEAVEN-EARTH

Directions

- *Inhale* as you bend knees slightly, curl arms, and tense all muscles; *exhale* as you move to stretch-balance position on either side.
- Begin by tensing as you bend knees and curl arms.
- Then stand tall and stretch one arm directly overhead as shown with opposite knee lifted to waist height and other arm down as shown.
- This movement can be done vigorously or slowly, for balance.
- Watch a spot in front of you to help balance.
- Advanced: rise up on the ball of your foot as you stretch upward.

Benefits

- Invigorates entire musculature.
- Enhances coordination and balance.
- Floods energy field with strength and vitality.
- Stimulates and integrates two hemispheres of the brain.
- Releases numerous points along energy meridians.

start   finish

LEG-SWING LUNGE

Directions

- *Inhale* as you swing one leg forward; *exhale* as you swing leg back — repeat three times.
- As leg swings forward for the third time, lunge onto forward leg as shown and bounce gently up and down in the lunge position three times with three sharp, full, exhalations.

- Rise up on forward lunge leg (so you are now balancing on opposite leg) and:
- Repeat all movements — (leg swings then lunge) on opposite side.
- Keep feet facing forward.
- Keep back and upper torso vertical during leg swings and lunge bounces.

Benefits

- Stimulates cardiovascular system.
- Increases power of legs.
- Provides stretch for thigh and Achilles tendon.
- Enhances coordination and balance.

- Coordinates right and left brain and body.
- Contributes to improved rhythm, timing, vitality.

3 swings   lunge

ARCH-PIKE

Directions

- *Inhale* as hips move forward; *exhale* as hips move back.
- As shown, use chair, couch, bench, bed, or other stable object.
- Keep arms straight.

- As you arch your back, lift your head gently, eyes looking up.
- As your hips push up and back, move head between shoulders and look toward belly, stretching shoulders.

Benefits

- Improves flexibility of spine and legs.
- Releases tension in lower back and abdomen.

- Strengthens shoulders and wrists.
- Opens solar plexus.

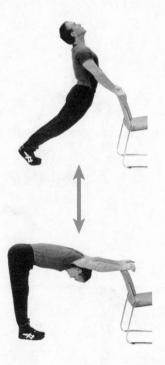

KICKBOXING LEG SWEEP

Directions

- *Inhale* as you lift leg up in front; *exhale* as leg sweeps sideward and back.
- *Inhale* once again as leg sweeps around from back to side to front.
- Repeat this sequence three times with each leg.

- Standing leg is slightly bent.
- Begin learning with leg held lower than shown — work up to waist height gradually.
- For balance, keep eyes focused forward and pelvis stable.

Benefits

- Tones upper leg, lower abdominal, hip flexors, and buttocks.
- Improves balance and coor-dination.

- Supports lower back and frees tension.
- Reduces injuries to hip connectors.

start

BODY-MIND BALANCE

Directions

- Sitting on chair, bench, or floor, with spine straight —
- *Inhale* letting belly expand; *exhale* as belly relaxes.
- Let any thoughts come and go but return attention to the rise and fall of your abdomen.

- Remain sitting as you count ten breaths, until heart rate returns to normal, or as long as desired.
- Enjoy a sense of centeredness, of equilibrium and serenity, and take that with you into your day.

Benefits

- Reestablishes normal metabolism as a transition back to daily activities.
- Provides rest, relaxation, and release.

- Relaxes and coordinates body and mind, enhances concentration.

front

side

The Evolution of Fitness

Before 1950, popular culture decreed that fitness meant big muscles. Men, with their larger bodies, were thus mistakenly considered more fit than women and the exercises people performed to become fit centered around strength and power. But, as a few people noticed, sometimes even bodybuilders died young. Big muscles didn't always help people feel better or live longer.

Then came the aerobics revolution, popularized by Dr. Kenneth Cooper and others, which showed that cardiovascular capacity — the heart, lungs, and blood vessels — provided a more meaningful indicator of fitness, vitality, and longevity than muscles alone. People began to think of women, who had started jogging, doing aerobic dance, and swimming, as equally or more fit than muscular men who lacked cardiovascular endurance. Popular understanding of fitness began to delve deeper into the body, beneath the muscular armor. With a new emphasis on aerobics — combined with some strength training — we began to pursue new kinds of exercise, such as jogging, aerobic dance, swimming, bicycling, and other forms of training that make moderate but persistent demands on the cardiopulmonary system.

Our understanding of fitness continues to evolve. Today we enjoy a growing awareness of the Eastern psychophysical traditions of training, such as yoga; internal martial arts, such as T'ai Chi and Aikido; and healthful disciplines like Chi Gong and a variety of hands-on and energetic bodywork. We are delving deeper into the innermost recesses of the body and mind — into the nervous system, and the controlling glands of the body.

Today we embrace the benefits of strength training *and* cardiovascular workouts. We are now beginning to appreciate the supreme importance of a centered, balanced, serene, and inspired state of harmony, where body, mind, and spirit form a holy trinity, a whole greater than its parts. And as our concepts of fitness change, so do our exercises. Where once strength training was supreme, we now pursue cross-training that incorporates aerobics *and* breathing, stretching, concentration, balance, and relaxation. And we now exercise body, breath, and attention in forms of dynamic meditation and sitting practice.

Meditation as a Fitness Exercise

At the highest levels of spiritual practice, meditation goes beyond the act of being aware, and enters the realm of *becoming awareness itself*. You become the witness who sits in serene balance, neither leaning forward into the future nor backward into the past. You sit, stable and detached, merely watching the body, mind, emotions, and soul — watching with the eyes of God.

For some, meditation is this profound, but for the purposes of body mind mastery, it may be more practical to view meditation as a revolutionary (or at least evolutionary) form of fitness training, essential to any complete workout — the ultimate cool-down.

If the deepest realms and rewards of fitness lie in calming and balancing the nervous system, focusing the mind, and pacifying the spirit, then meditation does this the same way push-ups strengthen the muscles or bicycling expands the heart and lungs.

Numerous medical studies show that those who practice meditation experience lowered or stabilized blood pressure, less stress-produced tension, and fewer stress-related maladies. The evidence also points to other productive behavioral changes, including a reduced tendency toward addiction, and even enhanced access to creative inspiration.

Instead of viewing meditation as an esoteric, Eastern religious practice, or placing it on a spiritual pedestal, we can appreciate it as we would sit-ups or jogging — as the next step up the stairway to our potential, on our journey to body mind mastery.

Learning How to Learn

You may have had the opportunity as a child to play in an empty lot just after a fresh snowfall, when the bare earth was hidden by a smooth blanket of snow. Maybe that winter you were the first kid on your block to blaze the first straight, clean pathway through the crunchy, knee-deep carpet of white. As it happens, the neurological pathways you blaze through your nervous system when you learn a new movement pattern are just like those paths through the snowy field. And the enjoyment can be just as great.

Once you have prepared well, you are ready to learn your new skill — to blaze the neural pathway. Repetition of the skill will serve to *groove* the pathway. This applies to any set of movements, simple or complex, whether running, jumping, swinging a racquet, throwing a ball, playing an instrument, turning a somersault, or singing an aria.

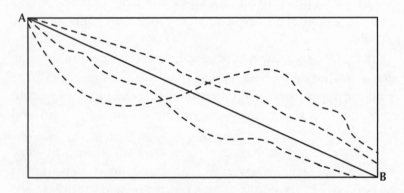

I use this image of the snow-covered lot above because it graphically represents what happens in your neuromuscular system when you are learning a new skill. The solid line from A to B shows the perfect execution of a skill. If line A–B is your first attempt at the skill, it means that you were totally prepared — mentally, emotionally, and physically — and were thus ready to perform it correctly the very first time.

Because most of us are not perfectly prepared, our first attempts are represented by the curving dotted lines in the figure. Then you gradually home in on line A–B. This homing in process takes varying amounts of time, depending upon the approach to learning.

Your first attempt at a new skill is most important, because you're forging a new pathway. The next time — and each time after that — you're likely to follow your first path. Every time you take this neural pathway, you'll stabilize and reinforce the motor response — whether or not it is correct.

Every time you let yourself practice a movement incorrectly, you're getting better at doing it incorrectly. It follows that you want to repeat the correct movement pattern as much as possible and to avoid, at all costs, reinforcing an incorrect pattern. A fundamental rule of learning, therefore, is *never repeat the same error twice.*

Errors are a part of learning; we all make them. But if you make different errors each time, you don't habituate yourself to any single incorrect movement pattern. This is very important, because one of the prime causes of slow learning is repetition of, and habituation to, an incorrect motor response. You get used to swinging the racquet or bat too low; you get accustomed to arching in a handstand; you begin to feel comfortable shifting your weight to the wrong foot on your golf swing.

By making each attempt different, you explore and experiment while homing in on the straight path, the optimal movement, and avoid grooving bad habits.

Awareness and Practice

If you practice hitting five hundred golf balls every day but really pay attention to only one hundred swings, then you're wasting four hundred swings a day. In fact, those four hundred semiconscious swings may do more harm than good, because, as I just pointed out, you can form incorrect pathways without

noticing it — like walking through the snow-covered lot in
your sleep.

Only perfect practice makes perfect. Proper learning technique consists not only of attempting the correct pattern but
also of avoiding the incorrect one. Remain fully aware in your
mind and in your body of every attempt you make during practice. If you make an error, don't automatically repeat the
attempt. Take a moment to fully identify the error, or you're
likely to repeat it. Then do something different.

The Stages of Practice

Many of us assume that to improve we have to practice skills
many times, right from the start. In reality, most beginners tend
to practice *too much* at first. As a beginner, you'll probably have
a low level of kinesthetic or "feeling awareness" at first. You
don't know what the correct skill should feel like. When first
learning a new skill, many repetitions may develop an incorrect
pattern. Instead, begin with a few very conscious repetitions,
maintaining intense concentration and interest.

Continue practicing while concentration and interest are
strong. But if you begin to repeat an error, or if interest and
attention fade, then stop and return to your practice later.
Practice is like gambling: you have to know when to quit. Only
repeat your skill for endurance and stabilization when you can
consistently repeat the *correct* pattern.

I recommend *practicing in threes*. Learning studies have
shown that we can maintain our best concentration for three
attempts; the fourth try is generally not as good. So practice
everything in threes, and then pause, reflect, relax, and take a
break before practicing another series of three.

Following this principle of threes, I taught myself within a
very short time to juggle. I'd try each progression only four or
five times each day. Working for five minutes a day, I taught
myself to juggle three balls within five days. Some people might
learn to juggle three balls in *one* day. But my method, aligned

with natural order and realistic psychological dynamics, will allow you to learn correctly. Many fast learners also pick up little compensations and poor habit patterns. They may learn the skill quickly, but they don't necessarily learn it right. Take the time to learn it right, and you'll save time. There's a big difference between learning and learning correctly.

Remember, as you practice, stop for a moment between three attempts. Check yourself, take a deep breath, shake loose, and relax. Feel awareness tingling through your body, out to your fingertips and toes. Feel your connection to the earth. Then continue.

Learning, then, is not just a matter of casually (or fiercely) performing a motion over and over. Instead, employ insight and concentration in place of mechanical repetition.

The following techniques and principles will produce a faster, more powerful learning curve:

Overcompensation

Overcompensation may be the single most valuable aid to rapid skill learning. Here's why: When you perform an incorrect movement pattern over a period of time, you become comfortable with that pattern. Any changes — even toward the correct pattern — will feel *strange* and will be more difficult.

Movement teacher Matthias Alexander tells a story about a young girl who limped up to the stage during one of his seminars and allowed him to work with her to straighten out her twisted, distorted posture. After a few minutes she transformed from an almost grotesque posture to one that looked straight and aligned. As she walked gingerly back toward her mother in the audience, she was overheard to say, "Look Mommy, I'm all twisted up!"

> *When you're wrong,*
> *what's right feels wrong.*
> — *Matthias Alexander*

Because we all become comfortable with established patterns of moving and acting in the world, and because changes — even improvements — feel awkward for a time, we tend to *undercorrect*. We stick "close to home" — to the old familiar patterns. If, for example, you're learning to hit a baseball and have formed a habit of swinging too high, you'll tend to continue swinging too high. Even if you know you should swing lower, you'll tend not to swing low enough, because it feels wrong.

Applying the law of balance means you need to *overcompensate* — to work *both sides* of the movement in order to find the center. In other words, make a determined attempt to swing *too low*. In fact, you would deliberately try to miss the ball for the next ten swings by swinging beneath it. Since we tend to undercorrect, in trying to swing too low you'll probably end up hitting the ball. After working both sides — too high and too low — you'll find the correct, centered place.

FASTER LEARNING THROUGH OVERCOMPENSATION

I'm going to assume that catching an object in front of you that you've thrown over behind your back is a new skill for you. Take a lemon or another sturdy fruit. Toss it from behind your back, up over your shoulder, catching it in front of you in the same hand. You can throw the object over the same or the opposite shoulder of the hand in which you hold the object. The main object here is to make conscious use of overcompensation. Work on one variable at a time. If you threw too far to the left, then on your next attempt throw too far right. If you then throw too far behind you, make sure you throw way in front of you. Then you'll find the middle. ∎

The principle of overcompensation — working both sides — applies to elements of timing, balance, accuracy, and force in every possible sport or movement skill. It also applies to finding balance in everyday activities like walking, talking, eating, or making love.

You may be reluctant to work both sides of a skill; it may seem like a waste of time to deliberately putt too short or too long, or to shoot baskets too far right after noticing you're usually too far left. Naturally, most of us prefer to do it right on the next try, not wrong on the other side. But those willing to work both sides equally will sharpen their skills in sport and life with more success and in less time than those unwilling to do so.

Ideomotor Action and Mental Practice

Your powers of imagination can help you enhance old skills and learn new ones. The interaction of mind and muscle makes this possible. In the negative sense, turbulent thought can impose muscular tension, as you've seen. But on the positive side, clear mental imagery can — even without actual movement — develop correct muscular responses. A simple experiment demonstrates this principle:

MIND MOVING BODY

Tie a small weighted object like a ring to a six-inch length of string. Let the object hang by the string, held by your thumb and first finger. Hold the string still, and then begin to imagine that the ring is swinging back and forth, back and forth. Continue to imagine this, and watch what happens.

Next, while the ring swings back and forth, imagine that it is going in a circle instead. See the results.

This test demonstrates the phenomenon of ideomotor action: that for any image of movement there is a subtle, corresponding muscular impulse. If you relax the body and imagine yourself performing a movement correctly, the muscles respond. Ideomotor action is a key principle behind mental practice. ■

The value of mental practice is well established in research. One study used sixty beginning basketball players split into three groups of twenty each. The first group practiced shooting baskets from the free-throw line, attempting a specified number of shots in a specified time for a period of two weeks. The second group was asked to practice mentally in exactly the same fashion — *imagining* themselves shooting baskets. The third group performed unrelated activities during the same time period.

Each group was tested at the beginning and end of their two-week practice. As expected, the third group didn't improve. Those who practiced mentally, however, improved almost as much as those who trained physically.

The moral of the study is not, of course, that you should begin practicing from the living room couch but that mental practice can be very useful as a supplement to physical practice. I gained a reputation as a natural when I competed on the University of California's gymnastics team, because I seemed to learn difficult movements "effortlessly" on the first try. What my teammates didn't know was that I would dream about those moves the night before and perform them in my head all day before actually attempting them. When I finally executed the movement physically, it felt as if I'd already done it many times. This confidence helped me to overcome fear, too.

In some situations, especially, mental practice has distinct advantages:

- It's absolutely safe — unless you mentally practice your golf swing while driving down the freeway.
- You can do it anywhere. (Well, almost anywhere. I once mentally rehearsed a trampoline routine while sitting in a dull political science lecture. As I closed my eyes and imagined myself going through my routine, my arms made twitching, waving gestures as I mentally twisted and somersaulted. I opened my eyes to see the professor and about a hundred other people in the lecture hall straining for a look at the poor guy in the front row having a seizure.)
- It's free. If you take those private lessons twice instead of three times a week, or an hour each day instead of two, you can spend the rest of your time practicing in your imagination.
- Mental practice demands and develops your powers of concentration and clear imagery. It's very easy to casually practice actual physical skills without real attention by letting your body go through the motions. But mental practice requires clear attention.
- Because mental practice can be free of error, there's no fear of failure.

But there are exceptions to this last rule, too. One of my gymnasts at the University of California consistently fell off the balance beam. As surely as the sun rose, she'd fall off. She fell on weekdays or weekends, rain or shine, in practice or competition, without discrimination.

One day, out of sheer desperation — for her safety and my peace of mind — I suggested that she try mental practice for a while. "Go through five or ten routines perfectly, in your head," I said, feeling that perhaps in this way she'd develop a good habit.

I busied myself with the other gymnasts until later, when I glanced over and saw her sitting there, brows knitted in concentration, eyes shut tight, whispering to herself, "Damn. Oops . . . oh, damn." Even in her mind she kept falling off.

You can practice mentally if you're ill or injured, or at odd moments during the day when there's nothing much to do. It beats thinking about your problems and can provide a winning edge.

Visualizing yourself performing well in competition will also serve to program yourself for success, since your subconscious mind doesn't differentiate between what you see with your mind's eye and your physical eye. Imagery is a way of creating a new reality.

Mental practice also explains the common phenomenon of athletes returning to a sport after time off only to find that their technique had actually improved. It also explains a great improvement in a skill on a Monday after an athlete had trouble with it on a Friday and took the weekend off. In just thinking about the movements, it's possible to improve, because you don't practice any errors. Mental practice is more efficient than physical practice.

The main requirement of mental practice is to stay relaxed so that no other muscle tensions interfere with your proper response. While practicing mentally you can lie down, or you can sit quietly. Of course, you have to have some kind of *feel* for the movement before practicing it in your imagination. Once you know how it should feel, practice it repeatedly in your mind.

Using mental practice — visualization, imagery, mental rehearsal — is another essential tool for success in sport and life.

Slow-Motion Practice

Slow-motion practice provides another key to body mind mastery by giving you the time to become acutely aware of every part of a movement, whether it's swinging a golf club or washing dishes, performing martial arts or a piano concerto. When you perform an activity in slow motion you amplify awareness of tension and relaxation and feel subtleties of coordinating body parts, weight shifts, and breathing that you miss when moving quickly. Slow motion enhances both the ease and speed of learning, because formerly hidden mistakes become inescapably obvious.

SLOW-MOTION EXPERIENCE

Test 1. Hold your right hand in front of your face, so that you are looking into your palm. Quickly move your right arm out to the side, turning your palm outward, and stop. Notice that you were aware of only the beginning and end of the movement.

Test 2. Now repeat the same sequence, but this time move your arm and hand in slow motion — as slowly as you possibly can. Let it take a full minute. Be aware of the relaxation of the arm and hand muscles. Notice how each finger turns; clearly see the different angles of your hand, as if for the first time.

In this test, you were clearly aware of the movement of your arm and hand in its entirety, from beginning to end. After a period of slow-motion practice you can actually move faster than before because in moving slowly you are able to notice and release tension that slowed your reflexes. And less tension means faster movement. ■

Slow-motion practice provides similar benefits to studying slow-motion instant replay films of training, except that you're not just seeing but sensing.

You can apply slow motion to virtually every sport or movement art, as well as to the movements of daily life. Try taking a bite of food or washing a dish or brushing your teeth in slow motion, even for ten seconds, and notice the quality of attention and release of extra tension.

In learning any new skill, remember the formula PSP: First precision, then speed, then power. Each flows from the next in their proper order. If you want power and speed, then practice precisely in slow motion. Slow down to speed up.

Not only does slow motion work, *it's fun*. And, like practitioners of T'ai Chi, you discover that in slowing down, you turn sport into a form of moving meditation.

The Beginning-and-End Method

Sometimes it isn't practical to work in slow motion — for example, in learning a cartwheel or a somersault. In cases like this, it's useful to pay special attention to a perfect beginning and ending position. You may not know where you are in the middle of a movement, but if the beginning and ending postures are correct, the middle will take care of itself. That's why so many coaches in tennis or golf, for example, emphasize the correct beginning and follow-through.

When you swing a tennis racquet or golf club, hold the ending for a moment. Check your balance, the position of your arms, head, and body. Beginning and ending positions form the basis of a consistent swing.

If you complete a movement and find that you're in the wrong ending position, move quickly to the correct ending position and feel it. The next time, you won't be quite as far off; again, move to the correct ending posture. Before long, you'll find yourself ending the proper position, and the middle will flow smoothly as well.

Part-Whole Practice

Any skill, like the functioning of your flashlight, is made up of component parts. If you want to find out why a flashlight isn't working well, you take it apart and find the trouble spot. It works the same for a movement skill. When I coached and taught beginning gymnastics at Stanford University, my students learned a surprising number of skills by breaking each skill into relatively simple parts — first the beginning, then the middle, then the end. Then they put the parts together. In learning forward rolls, they first learned to squat and reach forward, then shift weight to the hands, and push their rear ends rapidly up and forward. Then they learned the end part, rolling from their backs up to their feet. Mastering each part made the whole far easier to learn, and learn correctly.

Not only do students learn better by focusing on the components of a skill, they have more fun because they experience small successes every day, rather than struggling toward the entire movement. When climbing a mountain, define each step in the right direction as success. We learn the alphabet before we write words; it works the same in sport and life. Many small successes add up.

You can learn anything in simple and progressive increments — like walking across steppingstones rather than trying to jump over a wide stream. Master each part before attempting the whole.

Imitation: The Ultimate Technique

Children are masters of imitation, the most powerful and natural way to learn. It's how we learned walking, speaking, and other practical life skills. Everything and everybody has a mixture of virtues and weaknesses. I've never met a single person who didn't have at least one quality I admired. I've applied the saying, "Don't envy — emulate."

If you look for the good in everyone you meet, that person becomes your teacher.

We have no friends; we have no enemies; we only have teachers.
— Anonymous

To learn a skill, find those who are accomplished at the skill and watch them carefully. Study their movements, habits, facial expressions. As you watch them perform, imagine yourself moving in the same manner.

Your ability will improve with practice. Even the most creative painters began by copying. If you wish to copy a drawing of a master artist, you won't be able to reproduce it precisely at first, but with practice, your copying will improve. You can practice imitation anywhere or anytime.

To copy athletic skills, you have to prepare first; you can't imitate a power-lifter unless you've developed some strength; you can only imitate a ballet dancer's movements after developing the same suppleness and control.

I'm convinced that imitation is the master technique of learning because it works at the subconscious level. One body learns directly from another, without intervention of the intellect.

To make best use of your innate powers of imitation:

- Prepare yourself physically by returning to talent basics.
- Appreciate that it's okay to copy. Inspiration begins with imitation.
- Make sure you have good role models.

IMITATION PRACTICE

Have a partner face you. Have your partner hold his or her arm in an unusual position. Copy your partner's arm position, as if looking in a mirror. Then have your partner take another position, perhaps with both arms askew. Imitate that. Then mirror his or her posture. Do the same thing as he or she moves very slowly.

In this mime and acting exercise, you'll find that with a little practice you can mirror your partner precisely, and you can apply this ability to observe and imitate in your sport and life. ■

In this chapter I've outlined practical ways to learn more efficiently. Only you have the power to make the words come alive. If you use even a single one of these techniques to its fullest extent, it will enhance your game and enrich your life.

> *Children have never been very good*
> *at listening to what their parents tell them —*
> *but they never fail to imitate them.*
> *— James Baldwin*

CHAPTER EIGHT

Competition and Cooperation

It may be that the race is not always to the swift, nor the
battle to the strong, but that's the way to bet.
— *Damon Runyan*

Competition can bring out your best and your worst, develop your strengths and reveal your weaknesses. Competition provides opportunities to face our own moments of truth. Drawing the best from a man or woman, competition can be a model for positive, assertive, and realistic efforts in daily life. Athletes tend to be successful outside sports because they learn that life doesn't just hand us everything, that some people excel more than others, and that such excellence comes from preparation and work. Sports, as successful athletes know, can be a source of practical life lessons about action and reaction, effort and results.

The competitive experience can, at its best, become a form of moving meditation in which all your attention, free of random daydreaming, is focused in the present moment. It's also an enjoyable form of entertainment for millions of people, and a source of inspiration to many boys and girls.

But competition also has a shadow side: It compares unique human beings in extremely specialized arenas, quantifying the whole of their efforts with scores, times, and measurements. Competition divides the world into the dualities of *winner* and *loser*. Children who play highly competitive games emerge as losers more often than winners, despite our well-intentioned words of "it's how you play the game. . . ."

Sometimes we lose in our quest to win.

Competition tends to breed camaraderie among teammates but animosity between opponents. (Football has been called a game in which you feel really good about half the players on the field.) Before collegiate games, I used to see pictures of the opposing team posted outside training-room doors, with the words, "The Enemy" written below. At some events I've even seen athletes laugh or cheer when a member of the opposing team falls. Such practices encourage hostility in daily life, as evidenced by the way drivers treat one another and pedestrians.

> *When I played pro football, I never set out to hurt*
> *anyone deliberately — unless it was, you know,*
> *important, like a league game or something.*
> — *Dick Butkus*

Competition can reinforce a simplistic, black-and-white view of the world, with winning as the only valued goal. We constantly compare ourselves to others to determine our own relative worth. As Jerry Seinfeld once said, "Second place is the top of the loser's category."

Day-to-day improvement seems a more meaningful measure of achievement than who beats whom, but "most improved" players rarely receive recognition unless their improvement translates into winning the game.

> *The Way of the sage is to act but not to compete.*
> — *Lao Tzu*

The game of musical chairs is a good example of the way competition is instilled by our culture during childhood. In his book *No Contest: The Case Against Competition*, psychologist Alfie Kohn demonstrates that every round of musical chairs eliminates a child until at the end "only one child is left tri-

umphantly seated while everyone else is standing on the sidelines, excluded from play. This is one way we learn to have a
good time in America."

Most of us have played this game; few of us were trauma-
tized by not finding a chair, but you might remember the sink-
ing feeling. Sure, life is difficult, and we have to learn to deal
with disappointment, with losing sometimes. But what mes-
sages did that innocent little children's game teach us? That
there isn't enough to go around, so you had better scramble —
maybe even push someone else aside, because we'll either be in,
or out in the cold. Games reflect a society's needs and level of
awareness.

Kohn argued that as societies and our own sensibilities
evolve, we may need to create new games to meet the needs of
future generations. *No Contest* points to several hundred studies that showed how competition undermines self-esteem, poi-
sons relationships, and keeps us from doing our best. These
findings are particularly unsettling for athletes or parents. Most
of us, after all, assume that competitive sports teach all sorts of
useful lessons and accept that games by definition must produce a winner and a loser. But I've come to agree with Kohn
that recreation at its best does not require people to triumph
over others — indeed, quite the contrary.

Terry Orlick, a sports psychologist at the University of
Ottawa, examined musical chairs and proposed that you keep
the basic format of removing chairs but change the goal.
Instead, the children try to fit *everyone* on a diminishing number of seats. At the end, a group of giggling children must figure out how to squish onto a single chair. Everyone plays to the
end; everyone has a good time.

Orlick and others have devised or collected hundreds of
such games for both children and adults. The underlying theory
is simple: All games involve overcoming an obstacle to achieve
a goal, but nowhere is it written that the obstacle has to be
someone else. The purpose of a game can be for each person on
the field to make a specified contribution to the goal, or for all

players to reach a certain score, or for all to work with their partners against a time limit. In such games, an opponent becomes a partner. In these activities the entire dynamic of the game shifts, and one's attitude toward the other players changes with it. In contrast, competition leads children to envy winners, to dismiss losers, and to be suspicious of just about everyone.

Kohn might be encouraged by the game of "Effortless Tennis" originated by Brent Zeller, a gifted teacher who devised a natural, flowing, nonstressful, and cooperative approach in which the goal is to keep the ball in play as long as possible by hitting it to where one's partner can return it — thereby getting a better workout, with more volleys and improved skills.

The Competitive Mind

Looking critically at some of competition's liabilities doesn't mean that we need to do away with it. Rather, we need to explore the liabilities of the competitive mind.

And athletes don't have a monopoly on the competitive state of mind: essentially comparing one's performance to someone else's. The competitive mind emerges in every aspect of life — between siblings, partners, men, and women — even in noncompetitive arts like modern dance, ballet, or music, where we find jealously competitive performers.

I've known world-class athletes who viewed their work from a purely cooperative perspective. Steve Hug, a top U.S. Olympian in gymnasts, never really competed against anyone, because he didn't have that mindset. He simply did his best, measured by his own standards of excellence. Because of his approach, he was one of the most centered athletes and successful competitors I've known.

Even in one-on-one sports, such as tennis or boxing, you can view your opponent as your teacher and your student. You each do your best as you test and teach one another, revealing where your opponent needs to improve, as he or she does the same for you. Once we view competition in this manner, we can strive to do our very best, without succumbing to overtones of hostility and negativity.

When we overcome the combative state of mind, when we no longer have opponents — only people like ourselves, brothers and sisters in training, all striving toward excellence — we achieve the highest potential of sport. This is equally true in everyday life, when we compare and compete with others over who is the most popular, most attractive, most successful. The key, it seems, is to maintain a balanced perspective, appreciating the value as well as the pitfalls of the competitive mind-set in sport or life. It's not that people who maintain a balanced perspective never compete; they just don't take it too seriously. They remember that a game is just a game — and from their perspective, life, too, is a game.

The moment of truth itself, whether in performance or competition, can serve as an exciting stimulus to excellence. Yet its purpose ends when the race ends. Once we catch a fish, we no longer need the net; once we cross a stream, we no longer need the boat. And when the competition is over, we need not linger over scores, numbers, or statistics. We don't need to preserve past scores like prize butterflies. When we let go of our preoccupation with numbers, statistics, titles, and victories, we rediscover the sheer joy in *the process* of training, learning, and striving toward the heights of our potential.

Once the game is over, the outcome is history. Fame is fleeting, and glory fades. The only lasting value in the competitive experience is the lessons we learn and live.

> *It is not true that nice guys finish last;*
> *nice guys are winners before the game even starts.*
> *— Addison Walker*

As an athlete, you will always find those more and less skilled than yourself. As you continue to progress, avoid becoming preoccupied with distant goals, or you may miss the pleasure of the climb. Whether your path on any given day is clear or rocky, the only real measure of your achievement can be found in answer to a single question: "Have I done my best today?" All winning, losing, titles, and fame fall into the shadow of that question.

Overload-Cutback

One powerful way to prepare for a performance or a competition involves progressive overload followed by cutting back before the main event. This strategy has both physical and psychological benefits. If you are about to run a five-mile race and you ran eight miles through the hills last week, you're not only going to be physically prepared, you're going to feel more relaxed and self-confident.

Gymnasts, for example, complete twelve or more routines in a workout, so that even if they feel a little sluggish on the day of competition, the few routines they perform that day will seem easy.

Emphasize quantity for conditioning earlier in the season, then as the season approaches a peak, stress quality. The exact timing of the change in emphasis varies from sport to sport. The important thing is to do more in training than you'll need to do in competition.

The following overload techniques can all be useful:

- Training with extra weight, such as running with heavier shoes or a backpack.
- Going greater distances or faster than necessary — or up hills.
- Practicing without the use of one sense — eyes closed, for example — so that the other senses become more refined.
- Working under deliberately poor conditions. Jugglers, for example, may practice in dim light or windy conditions; ice skaters may train for a while on rough ice, in case they meet

these conditions in competition; martial artists may practice their skills in the ocean surf or in a pool underwater.

- Increasing the normal demand. A baseball batter, for example, can have the pitcher throw fastballs from three-quarters the usual distance. If the batter can learn to hit those pitches, connecting with full-distance throws will be far easier.

How much overload you practice depends upon your own temperament, capacity, and activity. The main point of the exercise is to practice some kind of overload, then cut back for competition.

Preparing Emotions and Attitudes

It's entirely normal to feel nervous before a competition. You may experience shaky knees, upset stomach, compulsive yawning, or other symptoms.

Understanding the nature of the precompetitive body helps to overcome — and use — the symptoms of nervousness. Remember that the competition is a ceremony, a special occasion when you are, in reality, tested. You *should* feel nervous! Your body is preparing for a unique demand: adrenaline is released into the bloodstream, stimulating a release of simple sugars into the muscles for extraordinary activity; your heart begins to beat faster; your breathing mechanisms are stimulated (thus the yawning). The muscles are trembling with readiness and energy.

Don't fight it — use it. Move around. Do some jumping jacks, run in place, or do a few push-ups. All of the body's responses are designed to enable you to move faster, stronger, and better — so *move*.

Before a competition I used to go into the bathroom, look in the mirror, and, providing I was alone, tell myself how well I was going to do. Then I'd do some shadow boxing, breathing explosively with each punch, a practice I recommend before any competition or performance, whether you are entering a playing field, concert arena, or business meeting.

Many thoughts and feelings, both positive and negative, may pass through your mind when the heat's turned up and the pressure's on. You have little control over thoughts and emotions. It's best to focus on what you realistically have more control over: your body. So in any stressful situation, remember to relax and breathe fully so you can channel and direct the extra energy. The only difference between fear and excitement is whether you're breathing.

The Mental Game

Competition or performance tests, demands, and develops all your capacities; physical skill is only one part of the game. It's not unusual for the most conditioned athletes to come in second or third because they haven't mastered the mental game. Even skilled athletes (or musicians or businesspeople) can fall short when their minds are distracted or emotions are in turmoil. The ancient samurai recognized that their minds had to be as razor-sharp as their swords if they were to reach old age.

Body mind masters treat training and performance with the same respect and intensity. When you train, you apply the same mental focus and determination as you would in competition; when you compete, you're as relaxed and easygoing as in practice.

Competition and performance offer the chance to show grace under pressure. And your attitude and behavior influence the attitudes and behavior of others. You have a chance to raise or lower the standards around you. All of us are teachers and examples, and believe me, people are watching. Psychological strategy can add a whole new dimension to competition and can turn a contest of brute strength and speed into a chess game. It requires mental acuity, refined judgment, and plain old intuition.

Your primary objective is to present your own best effort, not to sabotage someone else's. It's never helpful to psyche someone else out if, in the process, you too fall off-balance. You cannot control what they do, only what *you* do. The ultimate competitive strategy is to remain centered in your own unshakable spirit and calm. And even *appearing* as a tower of strength and confidence, whether or not you feel that way, is part of the game.

> *The only safe and sure way to destroy your enemies is*
> *to make them your friends.*
> — *Anonymous*

Above all, even as you play with your full determination and power, remember that the game will never be more than a game. The lessons it offers are important, but the game itself is only play.

In striving for body mind mastery, every day, every moment, is a learning experience, so ultimately, you can't lose. What better way to end this chapter than with a reminder from the Olympic Creed of 1894:

> *The most important thing*
> *is not to win, but to take part,*
> *just as the most important thing in life*
> *is not the triumph, but the attempt.*
> *The essential thing is not to have conquered,*
> *but to have fought well.*

CHAPTER NINE

The Evolution of Athletics

Unless you try to do something beyond what you have already mastered, you cannot grow.
— Ronald Osborn

Since ancient times, when athletes evaded charging bulls, fought lions, and hit rocks with sticks, sports have come a long way. Never static, sports evolve constantly, usually reflecting the dominant, mainstream values of the culture in their rules, structure, creativity, and tolerance for violence.

Some sports, such as ice hockey, approach the tradition of gladiators who often fought to the death for the entertainment of packed Roman stadiums. Other movement forms, such as gymnastics, sport acrobatics, diving, and ice skating, are evolving into performance art, with all the elegance and aesthetics of the ballet.

It's wonderful that such a variety of athletic forms exist to meet the interests and needs of different people.

But the sports we choose to play, both as individuals and a culture, warrant periodic scrutiny because of their power to shape our values and reinforce both negative and positive behaviors in our daily lives.

Sports and games can be fun, invigorating, and boisterous; they encourage teamwork, timing, cooperation, and organization. Athletes are stronger on many levels than nonathletes. We all recognizes the benefits of running, jumping, swinging, swimming, throwing, catching, somersaulting, and balancing. At the same time, the pressures of competition can cause chronic pain and injury. Sport can disable as well as heal.

Although the benefits of training far outweigh the liabilities, let's explore ways to enhance these benefits and diminish the liabilities.

You can ask two important questions about any sport:

1. *Does this sport contribute effectively to the physical and psychological well-being of the athlete?*
2. *Does this sport develop heightened capacity for daily life?*

With these two questions, you can look beyond a sport's entertainment value and assess its relative social value. And quite often changes are in order. Sports can evolve like any other institution to meet the changing needs and values in the modern world.

The records broken at each Olympic Games reflect new heights of achievement. Yet, from a spiritual perspective, we have a long way to go. In many high-pressure competitive sports today, athletes starve, overwork, overbulk, injure, abuse, or otherwise sacrifice their bodies by using steroids or other drugs in order to achieve short-terms goals. Faster progress is the all-important "victory." Such athletes have lost sight of natural law and the larger purpose of our lives. Self-destructive extremes represent a "moving violation" of the natural laws of balance.

Many favorite pastimes that involve one side of the body more than the other, including such games as tennis, bowling, golf, and baseball, create imbalances in the natural symmetry of the body. We shouldn't abandon these activities, but rather acknowledge, account for, and reduce their liabilities through wise training.

Today we are witnessing the birth of a new tradition in which sports are consciously designed for our overall well-being. Eventually we will replace the outdated games of the past with new and revamped sports that will better suit our changing sensibilities in the new millennium.

The most obvious way of changing sports is through modifications of the rules. The rules of today's sports have developed over many years. They reflect our views of what is fair and just and right; they indicate our current tolerance for violence and even our striving for beauty and spirit. Altering rules must therefore be undertaken with the greatest care.

With this in mind, I would suggest one basic rule change that would make our most popular games more interesting and challenging, and far healthier for our bodies.

Symmetrical Training

Golf, tennis, bowling, baseball, and many other sports that make primary use of one side of the body are marvelous games. As I mentioned above, however, they debilitate the symmetry of the body, and symmetry is vital for our natural alignment to the earth's gravitational pull. One simple rule change would improve their value and eliminate their major liability: requiring these athletes to use both arms equally.

There are several arguments against such a rule change: First, it would, in many cases, require equipment modifications. Second, today's stars would need to make some quick adjustments to remain stars. Third, those of us who were just beginning to feel proficient would have to undergo a temporary learning period again.

But here are the benefits of symmetrical training:

- You would enjoy a new and stimulating challenge.
- Chronic pain in elbows, backs, or shoulders would be lessened or eliminated by working both sides of the body, since each side would be given a periodic rest.
- You would end up a better performer. Research shows that learning a skill on one side increases learning facility on the other, and can help eliminate old weaknesses.

- You could practice longer without fatigue.
- You add greater versatility and dimension to your game.
- Your health and well-being would improve.

Re-Visioning Sports

The second and most important way you can personally influence the evolution of sport is by altering your own perception.

Casey Cook, an inspiring diver I coached at Oberlin College, told me that the sport of diving evolved for him as he began to view his movements in terms of energy awareness. He felt as if he were "sculpting" energy as he somersaulted his way into the air, forming lines of energy he could almost see. As he learned to shape the direction of energy flow, he felt he was playing a new game — on nature's team, with the board, the air, and the water as teammates. He was no longer a lonely body, bouncing on a board, mechanically spinning, attempting to knife through the water for a judge's reward.

During leisure hours, if he played baseball or threw a Frisbee, he continued to enjoy this sense of energy flow and graceful harmony with natural forces. Without a single rule change, Casey had changed the sport of diving by changing his perceptions.

Professional football player Chip Oliver quit the NFL at the height of his career because he realized that the sport as he had played it was harmful to the body or the spirit. After studying yoga and other integrative disciplines, Chip came to realize that, for him, football hurt too much. Later, Chip was drawn back into the sport he loved, but with a new approach to the game — using football as a means to blend with others, to practice symmetry, to master relaxation-in-movement, and to use the sport as a lesson in living.

Some of the mental, emotional, and physical benefits of expanding our perceptions to include the larger potential of a sport include the following:

Mental benefits
- Encourages the attitude of blending and harmonizing rather than collision; it presupposes no opponents or enemies, just teachers.
- Enhances ability to recognize the flow of energy.
- Demands and develops one-pointed concentration.

Emotional benefits
- Encourages friendly, cooperative interaction.
- Serves as a laboratory to understand yourself and others.
- Creates an atmosphere of mutual help and support through teamwork.
- Contains sufficient challenge to develop higher levels of courage, balance, and "grace under pressure," which carries over into everyday life.

Physical benefits
- Balances development of the body.
- Develops sensitivity to the body's needs instead of encouraging ignoring pain signals.
- Demands and develops suppleness of all body joints.
- Develops cardiovascular fitness and whole-body stamina.
- Aids muscular symmetry and postural alignment in gravity, balancing stresses on both sides.
- Enhances the body's connection to the earth through dynamic calm and relaxation-in-movement.

Every sport has weak or missing elements, so find compensatory activities to balance your game. If you are a football or ice-hockey player, you might take up T'ai Chi or hatha yoga; a tennis player might practice ballet; a musician might take up a martial art such as Aikido or karate.

Sample many sports and movement activities. If you, or your children, are exposed to a broad variety of sports and games, including dance, martial arts, and other activities, you will naturally find the form that works best for your (or their) interests, body type, and abilities.

There is no perfect game for you any more than there is a perfect soul mate or job or school. Everything has strengths and weaknesses, benefits and liabilities. Gymnastics, for example, offers impressive development of a wide array of physical qualities, but lacks the relaxed, socializing team interaction of baseball, while baseball doesn't come close to developing the gymnast's array of skills. Choose the game that suits your body, mind, and spirit.

New Games for New Lives

Master athletes don't seek victory at all costs. They recognize that ultimate victory means personal growth and long-range, lifetime benefits. So they naturally gravitate to new and experimental forms of exploration and fun. This section ends with a preview of sports to come, a vision of tomorrow. This list by no means exhausts the possibilities; and whether or not one is interested in practicing these sports below, they serve as examples of how any sport can evolve to better serve those who practice them.

SLOW-MOTION RUNNING
A New Approach

Object: To finish the race last.
Rules:
1. Competitors begin on the starting line, facing the finish, a wall, 10 yards away.
2. At the signal "Go!" all runners must begin to move continuously — without stopping their forward motion — in a direct line toward the finish.

3. Each step must be a length of at least twelve inches. (Measure by nine parallel lines, drawn between the starting line and finish.) ■

Slow-motion running is a far more challenging sport than it may appear at first. In trying to reach the wall last, the best athlete will have to move with awesome slowness. This requires excellent balance, sensitivity, ability to relax, and a kind of dynamic patience. The ability to perform in this way reflects an entirely new kind of psychophysical stamina, a quality of body-mind balance rarely explored in sports. Slow-motion running is a form of moving meditation similar to Zen meditation. If you try it, you'll appreciate how challenging and meditative it can be. It's a perfect counterbalance to the speedy pace of most of today's athletics.

T'AI CHI-DO
The Power of Synthesis

Object: Using slow motion to refine the movements of any practice — in this case, Aikido.

Rules: None as this practice is noncompetitive.

T'ai Chi-do incorporates the refined, slow motion training of T'ai Chi with the flowing, energy-blending qualities of Aikido.

T'ai Chi, which originated in China, uses, at beginning levels, slow-motion, softness, and sensitivity.

Aikido is nonviolent in intent — never designed to injure another deliberately — and emphasizes positive energy flow through relaxed movement. Practitioners deflect, channel, and control an attacker's energy through the use of graceful throws and wristlocks. Aikido contains a lighthearted blending of movement and energy and practice in falling and smooth rolling, which isn't included in T'ai Chi.

When thinking of self-defense, people usually imagine defense from an attacker. This imagery is limited. Through the practice of T'ai Chi or Aikido, one learns how to blend with everyday problems and stresses, from tension, fatigue, and lowered resistance, all of which attack us far more than human adversaries do. Aikido rolls are especially useful to people who may have occasion to fall and want to do it smoothly and creatively.

In the same manner you can combine slow-motion elements of T'ai Chi with another martial art, you can combine the positive qualities of other practices. ■

THE NEW GYMNASTICS
Efficiency and Fun

Object: As in other gymnastics events, to score as close as possible to a perfect ten on every event, through sufficient endurance and skill, flawless technique, and aesthetic style and presentation.

Rules:

1. Men's and women's events have been combined, so that men and women can compete with one another

on an equal basis. This is possible because, in gymnastics, athletes handle only their own body weight.

2. There are four events:

Floor-beam exercise. A combination of floor exercise and beam. A padded beam, 5 inches wide, adjustable between 2½ and 3½ feet high, is placed along the inside border of the padded, resilient floor-exercise area.

Each athlete performs a two-minute routine to musical accompaniment. In addition to the regular tumbling, dance, and floor-exercise work, the gymnast must travel the complete length of the beam 3 times, with turns, balance, and aerial elements, including a flowing mount and dismount for each passage.

Trampoline. A net-like bouncing surface allows any performer to achieve sufficient height. The trampoline is completely padded all around with a 6-foot border of 8-inch-thick pads, with the springs covered.

The performers engage in fifteen bounces total, judged on the basis of difficulty height, form, and control.

Double horizontal bar. The gymnast performs a horizontal-bar routine, but is required to pass through the air from one bar to the other at least three times during the routine. There is safety padding beneath the bars.

Sport acrobatics. Each team shows six routines of aesthetic pair work. Three routines consist of pairs of the same sex (male-male or female-female), and three routines are mixed pairs. Each routine is done in harmony with suitable music. Each routine must show balance, tumbling, dance, strength, all in tempo and in harmony with one's partner. ■

The new gymnastics offers a combination of mental and physical demands found in few other sports — an optimal combination of events to give the body balanced development. All four events are universal spectator favorites and consolidate the primary benefits of gymnastics: strength, suppleness, stamina, sensitivity, and, particularly, a refined kinesthetic sense. Men and women would be afforded the uncommon social opportunity to train together, as equals. And with less apparatus to buy, more programs could be set up around the country.

EFFORTLESS TENNIS

From Competition to Cooperation

Object: To keep the ball in play as long as possible, becoming a teacher rather than an opponent to the person across the net.

Rules: May be played as singles or doubles. The idea is to hit the ball so that the other players can return it while stretching their own abilities. ■

This approach to tennis is played in the spirit of mutual support rather than competition. Among its advantages:

- A better, longer-lasting aerobic workout, since volleys tend to be a lot longer.
- Faster improvement, because it involves more time actually moving and hitting the ball, as a result of longer volleys.
- Less stress; players maintain more relaxed bodies.
- Players of different skill levels and experience can play with one another because the game challenges beginners and experts equally.

THUNDERBALL
A Noncontact Martial Art

Thunderball is a noncontact martial art, game, and approach to life developed by Robert Morningstar, a T'ai Chi Ch'uan teacher in New York City. Partners pass from one to six balls back and forth in a flowing, circular fashion, without getting hit. The game provides

- a mirror of life that reveals our weak and strong links;
- a powerful form of body mind training;
- a doorway to inner silence;
- a perfect metaphor of relationship; and
- a sociable game for beginners; unlimited challenge for experts.

Form is everything. In Thunderball, skill comes naturally, with practice. "Thunderball sages" emerge through progressive stages, as in life. Begin with one ball, then two, and only later progress to three or more as the laughter begins. (Three balls = triples; four balls = wings over the world; five balls = catching a butterfly.) As you enjoy the spontaneous movement of Thunderball, master the following interconnected martial arts principles for life:

1. Breathe profoundly — no need to coordinate breath and movement; just let it happen.

2. Stay aligned/allied with gravity, feet at shoulder width; keep 70 percent of your weight on the ball of each foot and your spine erect. Avoid bending or twist-

ing awkwardly. Maintain parallel planes through ankles, knees, hips, shoulders, and ears.

3. Avoid getting hit. Step "off line" when necessary. Remain aware, yet empty. Be here now or get bopped.

4. Yield fully; offer no resistance. Harness momentum with pendular/circular movements. Redirect ball energy; do not "catch then throw." Practice nonattachment (avoid grasping, grabbing, or holding balls). Release multiples from same hand in which you caught them. Strive for silent movement — sound is a measure of resistance.

5. Train both sides of the body and mind equally. Don't switch hands. Eventually train both feet equally, too.

6. Cooperate. A player cannot "win" in this game without his or her partner. Attention to the three rings of harmony promotes flow, ensures "golden arcs" and prevents "shooting stars." It's okay to drop balls to catch others . . . what's to lose?

7. Remember the concept of relativity. By moving forward or backward in space, you can create or lose time. ∎

Thunderball produces a state of mental clarity and stillness from the very first few minutes of play.

Challenging at every level, for beginner through master, whether played with one partner or more, it differs from juggling in that participants do not catch and throw balls but rather return them without grasping, in a circular motion, using martial arts principles. Advanced practitioners have been known to handle as many as six balls at once! This art has to be seen to be appreciated and practiced to be enjoyed.

The uses and designs of sport are limitless. Since athletics is a mirror of daily life, you can bend your creative energies toward improving and evolving the benefits of conscious movement.

> *If the peak cannot be reached without losing touch*
> *with the body, or if it is reached through alienation*
> *of the body, then new games must be invented.*
> — *Dr. Michael Conant*

Athletics can be a means of enjoyment, recreation, psycho-fitness, biofeedback, or, as you will increasingly discover, a way of transcendence, of unity — a path to a spiritual life. The door is open. You have only to walk through.

The Aging Athlete

> *You know when you're getting old when*
> *you stoop to tie your shoes and wonder what else*
> *you can do while you're down there.*
> — *George Burns*

Each of us has a psychological clock — really a set of beliefs or expectations — that determines at what point you decide you're getting old. Maybe it's when you turn fifty, or when high school kids start calling you "Sir" or "Ma'am." Or maybe it happens when your first grandchild arrives, or you receive a newsletter from the Social Security Administration or the American Association of Retired Persons — all of which have happened to me.

At each of these points I've said, "Maybe it's time I slowed down; after all, I am a grandfather." Or friends will send me joke birthday cards saying things like, "After a certain age, any limbo contest could be your last." You begin to worry.

But then I read inspiring articles about athletes in their eighties, nineties, or hundreds who run 10K races, or do long ocean swims, pointing to the simple truth that *calendar age means almost nothing* in terms of your life, vitality, or fitness. Bernard Baruch once wrote, "'Old' is always fifteen years older than I am." Then I realize, we're not getting old — we're just getting older.

Some people are out of shape in their twenties, thirties, or forties; others remain fit into their eighties, nineties, and beyond. Different lifestyles, diets, and genetic predispositions create different rates of aging as measured by traditional variables.

It comes to this: You are as old as you feel, and you have an extraordinary influence over how you feel through your daily habits of activity, diet, and rest. Caring relationships, creative hobbies or career, and a sense of purpose and goals also enhance longevity and vitality.

Someone once observed, "At fifty, you are responsible for your face." You were born with a certain "face" or genetic potential, but by fifty, how you appear mirrors your lifestyle. We all inherit certain genetics, but your level of activity and other habits can greatly optimize or diminish your genetic potential.

Take the case of Dr. Ruth Heidrich, author of *A Race for Life: From Cancer to the Ironman*. In 1982, at the age of forty-seven, Ruth was diagnosed with breast cancer. She immediately researched every possible tactic to overcome the disease. After learning that breast cancer is often diet-related, she immediately embraced a strict vegan diet with absolutely no animal products. She went as far as to avoid foods that come in a can, jar, box, or bag, focusing instead on fresh and unprocessed fruits, grains, vegetables, and legumes.

Adopting a strict vegetarian diet, while a huge, positive step toward improved health for many, is not guaranteed to work miracles for everyone nor should everyone make this change. For Ruth, however, it worked wonders. She began to feel increased vitality almost immediately. Then she read about the Ironman Triathlon, with its 2.4-mile ocean swim, 112-mile bike ride, and 26.2-mile marathon. At first she thought it would be impossible for her. But then she realized that she'd been diagnosed with a possibly fatal disease and had nothing to lose but her life if she did nothing.

Today, more than a decade later, a trim and vital woman in her sixties, Ruth has run the Ironman Triathlon six times in three countries, as well as dozens of major marathons all over the world. She's run through Katmandu, Bangkok, Wake Island, and along the Great Wall of China. She holds numerous records and has won fifty races a year in her age group — sometimes two races on the same day. She holds a world record for her age group on the famed Cooper Clinic treadmill in Dallas, Texas. Her fitness level exceeds that of the clinic's superior fitness category for a thirty-year-old male.

Ruth Heidrich's story strongly suggests that your level of activity may be even more important than diet in terms of body mind mastery. She is living proof of the proverb, "To do something you love is to drink from the Fountain of Youth."

You don't need to run marathons to age gracefully and enjoy your golden years. It's important that you find a routine appropriate not only to your body but also to your interests and temperament. When I taught martial arts seminars, enthusiastic students would come up to me and ask, "There are so many martial arts. Which one should I study?" For more passive and introverted students, I'd recommend something outward and active, such as karate or Tae Kwon Do; I'd direct extroverted and assertive students to an "internal" art such as the slow-motion elements of T'ai Chi Ch'uan. This was just to help them find a balance. There truly is a martial art for every body and temperament. I believe T'ai Chi Ch'uan is ideal for older people to open and stretch the joints and ligaments, enhance balance, and reduce stress, while also increasing vitality.

Older people can practice any sport or game but need to begin, at least, in a manner appropriate not to their age but to their current level of vitality. In other words, begin where you are. Start with slow, easy, gentle exercise, for less time; stop *before* you feel tired, still wanting more. Then build gradually.

From the vantage point of a year later, you'll be amazed how far you've come.

It doesn't matter how athletic you used to be. (Another proverb: "The older a man gets, the faster he could run as a boy.") If you've been relatively inactive for years, your body may remember how to do the movements, but the joints and ligaments need a reintroduction. One injury can set you back for months; that's why I recommend a gradual progression (beginning with The Peaceful Warrior Warm-up).

Finally, know that any new demand on the body is an initiation that takes some discomfort, just as an airplane rising to a new altitude may hit bumps. You may feel more tired before you experience more energy.

Forget about your calendar age and do what is appropriate for your level of condition and energy. This is the easiest advice to give, but often the most difficult to take, because when you want to get in shape or lose weight, you want it *now*. So I offer one more reminder from Ben Franklin: "Those who can have patience, can have what they will." And one from Samuel Johnson, who said, "In a contest between patience and power, bet on patience."

Finally, remember that vigor and vitality is a matter of *activity*, not necessarily formal exercise. I'm always amazed to see cars driving around and around, looking for the closest space to the health club so they can get on a treadmill and walk three miles! Park the car at the farthest point from the store. Use the stairs instead of the escalator or elevator. Carry your groceries, garden, and do other activities that *keep you moving*. You will add more years to your life and more life to your years.

When sharks stop moving, they die; the same is true for people. (It just takes a little longer.) So continue to move, stretch, and breathe deeply whether you are doing deliberate, conscious exercise, or simply remaining active in everyday life. Body mind mastery doesn't end on the playing field or in the arena; it extends to every movement you make throughout your daily activities — how and when you sit, stand, breathe, and stretch in the process of daily living.

If you're going "over the hill" anyway, bring a kite! Think young, act young, move young. Become an ageless athlete in everyday life.

Mastering the Moving Experience

If one advances confidently in the direction of his dreams,
and endeavors to live the life which he has imagined, he
will meet with a success unexpected in common hours.
— Henry David Thoreau

Los Angeles, 1952. A new house was under construction on Redcliff Street. Up on the roof, atop the rafters, twenty feet above the street, stood a small boy, about to jump, staring down at a sand pile below, balancing precariously. I remember it well; that six-year-old boy was me.

Below, looking up, stood Steve Yusa, a boyhood friend and mentor — older, wiser, and, it seemed, far braver than I. He was, in my eyes, a supreme warrior; afraid of nothing, he met every challenge. With a shout, he would leap from that rooftop like the Vikings I had seen in the movies, leaping with sword in hand to the wolves.

Now it was my turn to jump, and my knees had turned to mush.

"Come on, Danny, you can do it."

"I don't know. . . ." I wanted to jump but stood there, trembling, for the better part of what seemed like an hour.

"Come on, do it!" Steve repeated. But I couldn't budge. Until Steve said something that changed my life: "Danny. Stop thinking and jump!" The next thing I knew I was soaring into space.

Twelve years later, in 1964, at the World Trampoline Championships in London, I rubbed the jet lag and two hour's sleep from my eighteen-year-old eyes and opened the door to the arena. Surveying the colorful scene, I saw nearly thirty trampoline champions from their respective countries, warming up, bouncing blurs of blue and yellow, red and green and gold, rocketing up, soaring skyward, somersaulting and twisting through the air. In four hours, one of us would be champion of the world.

In the end it came down to Gary Erwin, reigning NCAA champion, and me. I watched Gary's final routine; it looked flawless. I was going to have to pull out all the stops.

My legs felt a little numb and shaky as I started bouncing, higher and higher, preparing to explode into a twisting double somersault and begin my final routine. I experienced a flash of doubt; then, from a nearly forgotten rooftop, a voice echoed from the past: Stop thinking and jump! I stopped thinking and soared into space — to the championship of the world.

April, 1968. I joined my teammates in our quest to win our first National Collegiate Gymnastics Championships. The competition was one of the closest in NCAA history. In the end, it was all up to me, the last performer. My coach and teammates sat holding their breath and biting their lips as I chalked my hands and leaped to the horizontal bar.

The crowd was so hushed that the sound of my chalked hands sliding around the bar seemed the only sound in the arena; I knew that my teammates were going around the bar with me in their hearts and minds.

"Come on, Dan, you can do it. . . . Stop thinking, stop thinking. . . ."

A power beyond physical strength surged through me — beyond fear or doubt, with total focus and determination. I found myself performing a movement I had never done in competition before. Then, time stood still as I released the bar and flew upward, floating in the zone, somersaulting, seeing the ceiling, the floor, the ceiling. . . .

Everything depended on the landing; it had to be perfect. My body stretched open, dropping toward the mats. In the next instant, I knew — even before I heard the roar of the crowd, before my coach grabbed and shook my hand — I had done it. Yet "I" had done nothing. There was only that experience of everything happening, as if on its own — a moment bigger than I was, larger than life.

Those mystical moments in which you "see" lines of energy, feel what other players are going to do before they do it, or experience a oneness with others in the arena remind us that there is more to life, and more to ourselves, than we previously imagined.

Satori, the zone, and peak experience all provide a preview of our highest potential. As our field of training opens to reveal its secrets, its hidden potential, it becomes a vehicle for personal mastery.

Today, more than ever, athletes report extraordinary experiences, ranging from paranormal abilities and perceptions to moments of personal perfection, independent of whether they win or lose the game. Time slows down or even stands still, yet sometimes hours race by like minutes. In these special moments they feel a dazzling sensory clarity, the sense of being fully alive. Such peak experiences inspire us and call us to the ultimate truth of the athletic experience: that the varied forms of movement training are, as Bruce Lee once said, "different fingers pointing at the moon; if you focus on the finger, you miss the moon's light." We may hike up different paths, but we all climb the same mountain of body mind mastery.

This is a hero's journey, one in which victories are measured not by times or scores but by our progress on this larger quest. Spiritual training is a secret school. Spectators can watch and cheer the external battles; philosophers can ruminate about the trials and glories; but only those who have tasted it, who have reached out, leaped, danced, stretched, and sweated for it,

know the sweetness and promise of meeting the inner challenges. The spirit of the athlete was perhaps best expressed in
the words of Theodore Roosevelt, who said:

> It is not the critic who counts; not the one who points
> out how the strong stumbled, or where the doer of
> deeds could have done better. The credit belongs to
> those in the arena; who strive valiantly; who fail and
> come up short again and again; who know great enthu-
> siasm and great devotion; who at the best know in the
> end the triumph of high achievement; and who, at the
> worst, if they fail, *at least fail while daring greatly*, so
> that their place shall never be with those timid souls
> who know neither victory nor defeat.

The university remains the domain of the intellect; the temple is the domain of the heart; the gymnasium is the arena of
vitality. We each have the university, the temple, and the gymnasium within us. We humans stand at the last frontier, the
inward journey, as we discover the laws of the universe within
our own bodies — the path of the body mind master — as we
create true success in our sports, our arts, our lives. As in all
things, the reward is commensurate with the effort.

> *It is moving within*
> *a multitude of sensations and forces*
> *effortlessly, fluidly, without a trace of*
> *inappropriate exertion or tension.*
> *It is being danced by God at each moment,*
> *pirouetting, leaping, eluding all forces*
> *that work to trip up and snare the Dancer.*
> *— Robin Carlsen*

Our quests on the golf course, the playing field, the court,
the pool, or in the gymnasiums mirror the human journey.

Training is the path and the process, the means and end, a bridge to personal evolution.

As a world culture, we are learning the bittersweet lessons of material wealth and abject poverty, of excess and hunger, of amazing technology not yet tempered by wisdom. No longer satisfied with symbolic solutions, we seek both world peace and inner peace, a goal that waits beyond the intellect in that place where our hearts and minds open and find balance. In that balance are the secret teachings of this world.

The laws of nature, the laws of athletics, and the laws of living are one. There are no exceptions to these laws; we are both bound and liberated by them. The way of body mind mastery is the way of discipline without extremes; loving when we tend to withdraw from love; practicing unreasonable happiness by creating it for others with whom we train and live.

Rebirth of the Body Mind Master

Many of the athletes we see on television have reached a high level of physical fitness, but have not yet realized their full potential. At the Olympics, Wimbledon, or Pebble Beach, we see many experts but relatively few body mind masters. The following story illustrates the difference:

One day in feudal Japan, a master of the tea ceremony was running an errand in the marketplace and collided with a foul-tempered samurai. Immediately, the swordsman demanded an apology for the "insult" in the form of a duel to the death.

The tea master was in no position to decline, though he had no expertise with swords. He asked if he could complete his obligations for the day before meeting the samurai for the duel. It was agreed that they'd meet in a nearby orchard, later in the afternoon.

The tea master completed his errands early and stopped to visit the house of Miyamoto Musashi, a famous swordmaster and painter. The tea master told Master Miyamoto his predicament and asked if the swordmaster could teach him how to behave so as to die honorably.

"That is an unusual request," replied Miyamoto, "but I'll help if I can." Detecting an air of serene composure about the small man standing before him, Miyamoto asked him what art he practiced.

"I serve tea," he replied.

"Excellent! Then serve me tea," said Miyamoto.

Without hesitation, the tea master took his utensils from a pouch and began, with the utmost serenity and concentration, to perform the graceful, meditative ceremony of preparing, serving, and appreciating o-cha, the green tea.

Miyamoto was impressed by this man's obvious composure on the afternoon of his death. The tea master was apparently free of all thought about the fate that awaited him. Ignoring any thoughts of fear, he focused his attention upon the present moment of beauty.

"You already know how to die with honor," said Miyamoto, "but you can do this. . . ." Then Miyamoto instructed him how to die well, concluding that "it will probably end in a mutual slaying."

The tea master bowed and thanked the swordmaster. Carefully, he wrapped his implements and left for the duel.

As he arrived at the orchard, he saw the swordsman waiting impatiently, anxious to finish this petty killing. The tea master approached the samurai, laid his implements down as gently as he would a tiny infant — as if he expected to pick them up again in a few moments. Then, as Miyamoto had suggested, he bowed graciously to the samurai, as calmly as if he were about to serve him tea. Next, he raised his sword with but a single thought in his mind — to strike the samurai, no matter what.

As he stood, sword raised, mind focused, he saw the sword expert's eyes grow wide with wonder, then perplexity, then respect, then fear. No longer did the swordsman see a meek little man before him; now he saw a fearless warrior, an invincible opponent who had mastered the fear of death. Raised over the tea master's head, glinting blood-red in the sun's last rays, the samurai saw his own death.

The sword expert hesitated for a moment, then lowered his sword — and his head. He begged forgiveness from this little tea master, who later became his teacher in the art of living without fear.

Leaving the bushes from where he had concealed himself, Miyamoto stretched with pleasure, yawning like a cat. Grinning, he scratched his neck, turned, and walked home to a hot bath, a bowl of rice, and peaceful dreams.

Masters of one art have mastered all because they have mastered themselves. With dominion over both mind and muscle, they demonstrate power, serenity, and spirit. They not only have talent for sport, they have an expanded capacity for life. The experts shine in the competitive arena; the *masters* shine everywhere.

On the path of body mind mastery, physical skill mirrors our internal development. Master athletes may remain unnoticed by those around them because their internal skills are visible only to those who understand. Because they do everything naturally, they don't stand out. When observing them closely, you may note a certain relaxation, an effortless quality, and a kind of peaceful humor. They have no need to play a holy role. They have seen their lives upside down and inside out and have nothing left to defend or to prove. They are invincible because they contend with nothing.

Whatever they do, they practice; whatever they practice receives their undivided attention. They radiate security. Others follow, although the masters have no particular desire to lead. When they wash dishes, they only wash dishes; their minds become washcloths. When they walk, their minds are walking with them; when they cook, their minds are food on the grill; when they sweep, their minds clean the world.

Athletes practice athletics; poets practice poetry; musicians practice music. Body mind masters practicing everything, and create a ceremony out of every moment. They fold clothes, eat, wash their faces, stand, or sit with the same attention they might give a championship game. Their decisions have a three-dimensional quality, balanced between rationality, intuition, and gut instinct. Their decisions therefore always result in a natural and appropriate outcome. Ordinary, yet full of energy, force, and quality, they reveal the spirit of a peaceful warrior.

> *The body moves naturally, automatically, without any*
> *personal intervention. If you think too much, your*
> *actions become slow and hesitant. When questions arise,*
> *the mind tires; consciousness flickers and wavers*
> *like a candle flame in a breeze.*
> — *Taisen Deshimaru, swordmaster*

Masters serve as reminders that all specific practices are subordinate to the practice of daily life. Use natural law to master your training; use training to embody natural law.

Imagine yourself approaching the top of a mountain, feeling a growing internal alignment with the rhythms of nature. You round the last bend in the path in a state of satori, in the flow, in the zone, and see the peak before you. Then you notice someone standing there, smiling at you with bright, clear eyes — a master of daily life. You walk up to the master, filled with gratitude. As the master's face comes into focus, and you realize that the master is you.

About the Author

Dan Millman is a former world trampoline champion, martial arts instructor, gymnastics coach, and faculty member at Stanford, U.C. Berkeley, and Oberlin College. He is a member of both the U.C. Berkeley Athletic Hall of Fame and the U.S. Gymnastics Hall of Fame. Now a bestselling author and popular speaker, Dan presents practical ways to transform everyday challenges into vehicles of personal and spiritual growth.

His ten books have inspired millions of people in more than twenty languages worldwide. They include *Way of the Peaceful Warrior*, *Sacred Journey*, *No Ordinary Moments*, *The Life You Were Born to Live*, *The Laws of Spirit*, *Everyday Enlightenment*, *Divine Interventions*, and two books for children.

For nearly two decades, Dan's work has influenced leaders in all walks of life — including health, psychology, education, business, politics, entertainment, sports, and the arts — who share a common interest in the fields of personal growth and human potential. A youthful grandfather, he lives with his family in northern California.

**For information about Dan Millman's work,
visit his web site at www.danmillman.com**

If you enjoyed *Body Mind Mastery*, we recommend the following titles from New World Library:

Reality Fitness by Nicki Anderson. A refreshing antidote to slick promises that you can look just like the stars, this inspirational book is written by a personal trainer and mother of four to motivate and remind readers that any exercise is enough. (Coming January 2000.)

Yoga for Busy People: Increase Energy and Reduce Stress in Minutes a Day by Dawn Groves. This easy-to-understand primer takes the complex and sometimes enigmatic practice of yoga and breaks it down into three simple steps — all of which can be completed in the time it takes for a coffee break.

Meditation for Busy People: Sixty Seconds to Serenity by Dawn Groves. This small, supportive volume shows us how regular or even sporadic meditation can allow us to manage life's everyday demands with greater ease.

You Can Be Happy No Matter What by Richard Carlson, Ph.D. Most of us believe that our happiness depends on outside circumstances. Here, Dr. Carlson clearly shows that happiness has nothing to do with forces beyond our control — and, in fact, our natural state is contentment.

The Seven Spiritual Laws of Success by Deepak Chopra. Based on natural laws that govern all of creation, this book shatters the myth that success is the result of hard work, exacting plans, or driving ambition.

NEW WORLD LIBRARY is dedicated to publishing books and other media that inspire and challenge us to improve the quality of our lives and the world.

We are a socially and environmentally aware company, and we strive to embody the ideals presented in our publications. We recognize that we have an ethical responsibility to our customers, our staff members, and our planet.

We serve our customers by creating the finest publications possible on personal growth, creativity, spirituality, wellness, and other areas of emerging importance. We serve New World Library employees with generous benefits, significant profit sharing, and constant encouragement to pursue their most expansive dreams.

As a member of the Green Press Initiative, we print an increasing number of books with soy-based ink on 100 percent postconsumer-waste recycled paper. Also, we power our offices with solar energy and contribute to nonprofit organizations working to make the world a better place for us all.

Our products are available
in bookstores everywhere.
For our catalog, please contact:

New World Library
14 Pamaron Way
Novato, California 94949

Phone: 415-884-2100 or 800-972-6657
Catalog requests: Ext. 50
Orders: Ext. 52
Fax: 415-884-2199
Email: escort@newworldlibrary.com

To subscribe to our electronic newsletter, visit
www.newworldlibrary.com